When the Whole World Tips

When *the* Whole World *Tips*

Parenting through Crisis with Mindfulness and Balance

Celia Landman

Parallax Press
2236B Sixth Street
Berkeley, CA 94710
parallax.org

Parallax Press is the publishing division
of Plum Village Community of Engaged Buddhism, Inc.
© 2023 Celia Landman
All rights reserved

Cover and text design by Jess Morphew
Author photograph © Todd Della Bella, Della Bella Photography
Printed in Canada by Friesens on FSC certified paper.

Pali terms for Buddhist concepts are frequently used throughout this book. Some accents have been included to aid pronunciation.

ISBN 9781952692550
Ebook ISBN 9781952692567

LCCN 2023030631

1 2 3 4 5 FRIESENS 28 27 26 25 24 23

This book would not be possible without the guidance and insight of all my moms: Elizabeth, Norma, Joanne, Judith, Natalie, and Jori. Your nurturing, love, and teaching have changed my life.

Contents

Introduction

> Right Mindfulness is like a mother. When her child is sweet,
> she loves him, and when her child is crying, she still loves him.
> Everything that takes place in our body and our mind needs to
> be looked after equally. We don't fight. We say hello to our feeling
> so we can get to know each other better. Then, the next time that
> feeling arises, we will be able to greet it even more calmly.
>
> —THICH NHAT HANH

This book addresses the fundamental struggle of parenting: loving someone and being powerless to keep them from pain. The ancient Buddhist practice of equanimity, which I call loving and allowing, can give us a way to come home to our ability to love without losing ourselves in suffering. Allowing is not being permissive or passive, nor is it resisting or denying. It is understanding the whole of my experience with a heart wide enough to hold the suffering of my child, and myself. This balance creates a spaciousness able to include everything and to embrace feelings of helplessness and fear while being willing to continue trying.

My story as a mother is made from my children's experiences. In the words of one of my primary teachers, Zen master Thich Nhat Hanh, we cocreate each other and our relationship. They create me as a mother, and I create them as children. I am not separate from them. When I started writing this book, I asked my daughter for permission to share her story. Much of the time when she was growing up, I didn't talk about her struggles with depression, anxiety, or suicidal ideation and attempts because it could have created a stigmatizing mark on her. Children with depression and self-harm histories struggle with being seen as different and unreliable by others, who often watch them for any signs of shifting into that gray area of pain.

Stigmas surrounding mental health conditions are alive and thriving. In a country where, according to the National Institute of Mental Health, suicide has been the second leading cause of death for young people starting at age ten,[1] we have a lot to talk about. For me, talking about the adversities of having a child with mental health challenges and the path to find balance is an effort to start the healing. This healing includes parents who feel responsible and blamed for their child's mental health or invisible disabilities, from ADHD or autism through depression and all the way to high-risk behaviors or a compromised immune system. In all moments of caring, there is a need for parents to stay balanced in the midst of struggle, heartbreak, and pain.

I've experienced implied judgment and censure around my child's behavior, which adds to my burden of care and distances me from necessary support when I am feeling scared and alone. Parents need a safe place to talk about the many emotions that parenting a child in distress can bring up. It is acceptable to speak about fear, love, and helplessness, but dangerous to speak about the rage that may come from countless frustrations, about the dissatisfaction of losing freedom and autonomy while caring for an ill or compromised child, or the disappointment of missing out on the healthy, happy child that was wanted and expected. At times in my life, I've encountered so much pain I questioned why I became a parent. It's not a truth that's pretty, and I know I am not alone in feeling it.

I've included, along with my own stories, parenting reflections from members of the meditation community (called a Sangha) I belong to. The names have been changed to protect their identities. I didn't look far for these stories, and I believe every parent has experienced some form of suffering when their child was unwell. You may be suffering right now, or you know someone who is. This book, though, is not only for the moments when the world tips and the ground beneath is suddenly gone; it is also a training manual, to be used in relatively calm and peaceful phases that offer time and space to begin the work of reclaiming your own balance.

This book shares wisdom from the three limbs of Buddhism: early Buddhist texts from the Theravada (the wisdom of the elders), the gentleness of Vietnamese Zen, and the compassion of Tibetan Vajrayana. These teachings have helped me find the qualities of solidity, compassion, patience, wisdom, and strength in the face of uncertainty and doubt. You will also find a focus on the practice of equanimity and meditations that have given me (and others) perspective and stability. Entering into a meditation practice by using the practices offered in this book can greatly help train the body to experience the feeling of safety in the midst of chaos and uncertainty.

I use the words *practice, practitioner,* and *practicing* often in this book. For me, these words signify both the effort of integrating specific teachings and the impact doing so can have on our lives. These words demonstrate that what we do has an effect. If I am a musician, I practice translating the written language of music into a living experience, and I get better at doing so over time. In the same way, I get more skillful at transforming the stuck and painful places in myself when I practice. When I remember to attend to my body, my breath, and my feelings, and to balance myself with the laws of reality, I transform information into a cellular, lived experience that makes all the learning worthwhile and valuable. Such attention is a practice to return to, again and again. I practice meditation; I am a Buddhist practitioner. I practice living in accordance with the mindfulness trainings in Buddhism. I am certainly not perfect, but I put in the work and, most importantly, I bring willingness. I am not a perfect Buddhist. I am a practicing Buddhist.

This collection of learnings is not a packet of ancient wisdom to agree or disagree with, but a how-to manual for you to refer to and use in a very practical way. It is in doing these practices, in making a real and sustained effort to extend understanding, forgiveness, care, and compassion to yourself and your circumstances, that you will meet your life. As you read this book, pause, put it down, and try out the practices.

You will notice this book contains parenting stories that can stimulate pain. These stories are hard and important; walking beside these parents can show us ways out of pain. It can give us solidity and let us know we aren't alone. Our shared stories can transform our pain and give meaning to our suffering. It is my hope that this book can open a conversation about the legitimacy of all the feelings involved in parenting. That is the first step in transforming painful emotions—allowing them to be seen with understanding and fearlessly acknowledging the truth of what our lives are like while cultivating the compassion and wisdom to know that these fierce, painful feelings are not who we really are.

Our society is just waking up to understanding trauma as a response to any powerful or alarming experience during which we were not accompanied or safe. Trauma therapist and healer Resmaa Menakem writes, "Trauma is not a flaw or a weakness. It is a highly effective tool of safety and survival. Trauma is also not an event. Trauma is the body's protective response to an event—or a series of events—that it perceives as potentially dangerous."[2] There are stories shared here that hold trauma. I also offer many meditations in this book. If, when you meditate, you find yourself disassociating from the body, shaking, sweating, experiencing nausea, stomach pain, or intrusive flashbacks from the past, this may indicate trauma.[3] In this case, please pause to consider how you would like to proceed. Meditation with the guidance of a mental health provider trained in trauma integration can help slow things down and provide support for staying present in the body so the traumatic experience can be metabolized.[4]

It's also possible that meditation isn't helpful for you right now. I have a dear friend who developed PTSD after discovering her teenage daughter unconscious following a sleeping pill overdose. For her, meditation creates greater agitation because of reoccurring images and thoughts that arise. She can go into a full-blown panic attack from sitting in meditation. Talking with a trusted mental health provider, attending support groups, and being in the company of caring family and friends is a better way for her to calm her nervous system and gradually integrate intrusive images. Pay attention to what is supportive for you. The Buddha continually urged his followers to "come see for yourself" and not to take things on faith or simply believe the words of those in power. Trust your own wisdom and the wisdom of your body to guide you.

I wish all children abundant protection and care. A reliable and capable adult presence, particularly one that is balanced and steady, can instill feelings of safety and security in children. How can we offer care to children if we, the adults, don't have solidity and balance in ourselves? If you are reading this as a life raft when the sea of pain is swallowing you, it is my hope that you can find your footing again, regain your sovereignty, and know that there is strong earth beneath you—always. You can find your center when the whole world tips.

CHAPTER ONE

The Path

Listen. When everyone you love is gone, when everything you have has been taken away, you'll find the Path waiting underneath every rock on the road. These are the words of Kisagotami.

—Kisagotami (Skinny Gotami)

In My Life: My twenty-three-year-old daughter had a relapse in December 2022. Her boyfriend convinced her to seek treatment after she stockpiled poison and wrote good-bye notes. I visited her the day she was admitted to the hospital. In the windowless consult room, she looked small and crossed her arms protectively in front of her like a shield. "I am not going to feel this again," she said, her voice jagged with determination. Bella's relapse was her third admission to a hospital for attempted suicide in the last seven years. All three attempts have been in December. Even though this wasn't her first time on the ward, and by now I had years of practice building balance and stability in my life, I was shaken to hear her say, "The only reason I didn't do it was that it wouldn't have worked."

I had grown up believing if I put in effort, I could get what I wanted. I believed that when it came my turn to parent, I would get it right. I'd listen to my child. I'd be close to them. I'd have a relationship unlike that of my parents, or their parents. Mine would be based on consideration and unconditional regard. It would be lovely, sweet, and most likely easy because I would be so in sync with my child's feelings and needs.

Before having Bella, I had planned to bring her to work with me as an infant. Since I worked for myself designing and manufacturing a jewelry and gift line, it would be perfect. Bella would lie peacefully in a bassinet and sleep or play with toys while I talked on the phone, made samples, or had production meetings. I'd smile at her and hold her in my arms as I walked around the studio, showing her off to my staff. She would be adored, and the women who worked for me would help me care for her. I knew babies cried. I had helped raise my four younger siblings, so I knew about diapers and feeding and baby maintenance, but my baby would be different. My baby would be just like me, except tiny and cuter. She would be portable, sweet, and happy, a delightful companion who would learn and grow and be amazing.

And then I had a baby, and all of my ideas changed. Partly due to the taboo against speaking the truth about the unrealistic and paradoxical expectations of parents, my expectations had been wildly out of line with reality. It hasn't been safe for parents to speak about the pain of parenting suffering children or feeling like the demands of parenting are more than they can handle. Instead, most of us encounter countless reminders of how parenting and love are supposed to look and how selfless parents are supposed to be. These reminders may be endless online photos of holiday togetherness, smiling families, or healthy children and parents who look amazingly well rested and serene. This online imagery is vastly different from what a relationship really entails. Sometimes, because of what's happening with my children, I am pushed to despair, helplessness, frustration, and rage. I know my own balance and capacity directly affects my children; I've learned over and over during more than two decades of parenting that the most helpful work I can do for my kids is within myself.

Visiting my daughter on the psych ward that first week of December 2022, I felt guilty I hadn't seen her relapse coming. Bella had come home for Thanksgiving two weeks before and was smiling, busy, and productive. I've learned to watch for her silence and stoicism. When she stops laughing, I get concerned. But she wasn't like that. I didn't know how it all unraveled.

Her boyfriend told me later that Bella had been struggling for three months—getting more anxious, irritable, and not sleeping. He had been trying to keep her regulated. I wished it had been different, I wished someone had spoken up or reached out. When I saw Bella, she was agitated, frustrated, and trying to get discharged. "I've made a mistake. I need to go. This isn't for me." She was determined to leave the facility because she couldn't do her schoolwork. I spoke to the head nurse on duty, who agreed to allow Bella time to work on her laptop so she wouldn't get more anxious about graduate school. I stayed calm—an ability developed along with my spiritual practice over the last twenty-five years. I acknowledged to Bella how frustrating it was to be there and not to have access to her schoolwork. She agreed to stay until the next day to meet with the psychiatrist and get new medication but made no guarantees beyond that.

As I left the ward, I felt a moment of relief, and I knew that each step forward would be hard. Sitting in my car, a wave of anguish passed through me as I acknowledged that my child was ready to poison herself. I cried, and I felt the sadness and pain of loving someone who does not love themselves. I wanted Bella to be healed and whole more than anything, and I knew I did not have the power to make that happen.

When I first encountered this pain and felt my own groundlessness, I thought it would take my life away with it and leave me always uncertain and scared. But now I had a support system that I'd lacked in those earlier days. I told myself, *I am here for you, no matter what. I am here for the sadness.* I breathed, and this made space to hold the feelings I was experiencing: my fear, my hurt, my desire for all this to just be over and for Bella to be different. Each feeling came, and I knew, *Sadness is like this ... blame ... judgment. It feels like this.* I've learned that all these feelings hold a message, and my job is to make space to listen.

I got more support to help me stay steady so I could listen to myself. I called my empathy buddy, who picked up right away. My voice broke as I asked him if he had time to listen. "Celia needs me," he told his friend, and stepped outside. I told him where I was, what I had been doing, and how I felt, and he listened. He made space to walk with me and accompany me. We spoke for about twenty minutes, and I felt cared for. I called my sister that night too, and the next day a friend who has been through her own child's suicide attempt. I also talked to another, more experienced mother, who offered me understanding about how hard it is right now.

Every day, I accompanied myself in meditation, and I connected with someone who could listen in a nonjudgmental way. I sought out people who have enough balance to stay present in the midst of my grief. They offered me their equanimity, and I suffered less because of them. It is a gift for me to have these folks in my life—people who can hear my pain without attempting to fix the unfixable. It's a gift to have learned how to be more and more solid in the face of uncertainty and doubt, how to abide in a place of loving and allowing all my emotions. With these gifts, I am stronger and more able to take action—I don't have to run or hide from any feeling or situation. This is the fruit of my practice: the ability not to abandon myself. I am powerless to change what happens in my child's mind, but I have a choice about how I hold her pain and my own.

I didn't choose to be on this roller coaster of emotion. I didn't choose this path for my daughter or me. It wasn't what I ordered or wanted, and yet, it is my life. My heart breaks over and over, and each time it breaks, I am amazed to find more space to hold the suffering of parenting a child whose life is balanced on a thin line of regulation. In this book, I share wisdom that has supported me and others on this path. My wish is to offer reassurance to parents that even though there is fear and heartbreak, there is also an earned calm. The teachings I present, some ancient and some everyday common sense, are here to let you know you aren't alone. You didn't do something wrong, and you don't deserve punishment. These words and practices are here for you, to help you realize your steadiness in the midst of your child's pain.

Why Buddhism?

You do not need to be Buddhist to read this book or to do the practices. In fact, I've learned that labeling myself as anything can create unrealistic expectations and get in the way of showing up authentically. As a child in Massachusetts, I grew up in a house with three religions. I had an intensely Catholic mother who, also in her forties, began to practice meditation in the Insight Buddhist tradition and a nonpracticing Jewish–Tibetan Buddhist father. Both of my parents had deep spiritual values. My father's worldview and stability were informed by Buddhism. I saw my mother living in alignment with her spiritual values: she made time for prayer and contemplation despite the disorder and unpredictability of life. She leaned on her faith, and it supported her.

Due to my mother's adherence to Vatican rules, my parents had six children in nine years. I was the eldest girl, with one brother thirteen months older. In a house with six children, there was plenty of daily chaos, noise, disorder, and enforced togetherness. In the 1970s, an era of benign neglect, it wasn't unusual for parents to open the door in the morning, eject the kids into the neighborhood, and see them only for lunch and dinner. I grew up visiting my neighbors' houses, especially the ones who would give us snacks or candy. I spent the day playing with other kids, only coming home when my mother yelled, "Tom, Michael, Celia, dinner!" I remember my mother mostly as an indoor dweller, taking care of the littlest children. She was the one who entertained us when it rained, kept peace during daily disputes, made meat loaf, disciplined us with a wooden Dr. Scholl sandal, and bathed and fed us. My mother was almost always worn out. I became "the little mommy," helping take care of her so she could take care of us.

My father supported our clan by working as an English teacher at a state university. He dreamed of being a poet and living a life devoted to esoteric, lovely things, and yet here he was, teaching freshman English to apathetic kids who just wanted to get their English requirements out of the way before moving on to computer courses. My father was disappointed to be living a life so out of line with what he had wanted for himself. He longed for freedom and a sink without dishes, for a place where he could study Chaucer without hearing fighting kids or stepping on toys and tangled clothing: somewhere he wouldn't have to work so hard or feel so trapped. It was a daily struggle to meet basic needs on his assistant professor salary.

I was five when my father began to rage. There were four kids in the family then, and my guess is that the responsibility felt overwhelming to him. His anger increased with the next two births; I remember daily rages that left me feeling shaky, terrified, and like I wanted the earth to open and cover me. I didn't feel safe or at ease in the house. I got used to wanting the ground to swallow me up so that I could avoid the shame of blame and humiliation. Since my father was the only Buddhist I knew as a child, I thought Buddhists were irate, quick-to-anger folks who wanted nothing to do with the sordid mess of us unenlightened ones.

I now have huge compassion for my father and the pain he endured. I now know that his rage came from his own past and from not having the life or the support he wanted. I also know that his rage was abuse. I carry residue from his outbursts and his mercurial moods. I see how being in the scope of my father's anger marked my life. I developed the habit of freezing when I encountered someone's anger. I wanted to disappear. Anger meant I wasn't safe. It meant I was wrong and unlovable and didn't belong. Although my responses have softened over the years, I still have this powerful protector in me who finds it hard to be near someone else's anger, even when it has nothing to do with me. I know the power that anger carries, especially with children, and I didn't want to transmit the legacy I had received. The effects of living with rage can last a lifetime.

After living through my father's rages, it took years for me to see that Buddhism contained a heart larger than anything I imagined. My path toward Buddhism and to equanimity practices for parents developed because of my kids and my desire to bring a spiritual tradition into our family life. Even though it was inconsistently modeled, I had grown up seeing how faith could bring solidity and peace. As a new parent, I investigated Lutheranism and Judaism, but the language of patriarchy and compliance in these theistic traditions made me squirm. I had an aversion to joining an organization that created an "us and them," believers and nonbelievers. My mother said I was throwing out the baby with the bathwater, leaving what was wholesome and supportive because I disagreed with the packaging, but to me it felt more like putting on a scratchy sweater and pretending it wasn't giving me a rash.

It was during a Sunday service with the Unitarian Universalists that I learned about Buddhism. The guest presenter that Sunday, Charlie, was a practitioner in the Plum Village tradition, the Vietnamese Zen lineage popularized by the soft-spoken and gentle Zen master Thich Nhat Hanh—affectionately dubbed Thay, Vietnamese for *teacher*, by his students. Charlie presented the teaching that the mind is like a field full of seeds—seeds of happiness, unhappiness, anger, dissatisfaction, love, and joy—all planted below our level of consciousness. He explained that these mental seeds grow with our intentions and attention, rather than when given water and sunlight. When I give my attention to my anger by yelling, screaming, hitting, hiding from, or avoiding anger, I let the seed of anger in me grow big and strong. With attention and action, the seed of anger can grow into a powerful and toxic plant. When I hold anger with mindfulness and embrace it with compassion and understanding, the seed doesn't sprout: when the feeling is accompanied, it returns to rest beneath the soil, harmless once more. The same is true for seeds of happiness and joy. If we water them with care and attention, they grow into healthy, vibrant, and beautiful flowers that we and others in our lives can enjoy.

This way of engaging with emotions and intentionally accepting and caring for them was new to me. I had thought all Buddhists were removed and detached, preferring not to get into the dirt of relationships and feelings. The last question Charlie asked that day was, "Do you want more happiness in your life?" Sitting in my seat, I felt the answer with my whole body: Yes. I longed to feel happier, safer, and more at home in the world. I wanted to feel belonging, to be accepted with all my scratchy and broken places, to be myself and know that whatever I felt was okay. I never knew there was a path to get to that place. Now I could see there was a way to get there.

Practice: Meeting Myself

One of the first things I learned about Buddhism was that it includes the body. It's easy to get pulled into fear or speculation and to lose our center when our children are in pain. When the mind moves into anxiety, the body comes along. We may not realize how much tension and worry we hold in the body; consciously relaxing the body can help us to notice when contraction occurs. It's impossible to feel safe and solid in a body that is fearful and contracted. Actively practicing physical relaxation and acceptance has the power to reestablish presence for ourselves.

For years, I've done this practice in the car before I drive. When I have passengers, I tell them, "I am going to take three breaths before I drive." Sometimes they breathe along with me. If they are teenagers, they give each other wide-eyed looks. This breathing is so much a part of my driving pattern that when I was teaching my daughter, Bella, to drive I asked her, "What do you do first?" and she answered, "I know, take three breaths." I was looking for "adjust your rearview and side mirrors" and was surprised and happy that she had taken in this breathing practice through my example.

In just three breaths we can practice stopping, calming, and healing. We can practice this every hour, every half hour, every fifteen minutes, or every time we get in the car. Using the Mindfulness Bell or Insight Timer app may be supportive—setting timers throughout the day gives us permission to stop and enjoy the experience of safety in the midst of what may not feel safe.

EXERCISE

Invitation to Practice Three Breaths to Presence

It is hard to meditate and read at the same time. Many of these meditations are recorded and on my official website. For all meditations in this book, my recommendation is to read through the meditation once and then try it on your own, reading along as necessary. Another option is to record yourself reading the meditation and then play it back whenever you'd like to practice. Alternatively, finding a practice partner and taking turns reading to each other could feel connective and supportive.

Begin by inviting yourself to rest in a comfortable supported position, seated, standing, or lying down. The eyes can be closed or softly focused on something that is restful. As you breathe, invite the following phrases to accompany your inhales and exhales:

1. Breathing in, I am aware of my body.
   Breathing out, I release any tension in my body.

2. Breathing in, I am aware of my mind and emotions.
   Breathing out, I accept and say, "Of course" or "I understand."

3. Breathing in, "Here."
   Breathing out, "Now."

Repeat as often as you'd like. This sequence helps to create a spaciousness capable of holding and accompanying mental and physical pain and joy. It can lead you home to a place beyond busyness or discomfort, to a solid place inside where you can return whenever you like. Touching into this place of wholeness and dependability even when our kids are in distress, we become our own refuge.

What Is Mindfulness?

I work as a mindfulness educator. I have a master's degree in Mindfulness Studies, which means folks give me a quizzical look and ask where I teach yoga. I explain that I like doing yoga, and that yoga is a physical way to experience mindfulness, but that I don't teach yoga. I think of mindfulness as an intention to meet myself and my situation just as it is. As Thich Nhat Hanh says, mindfulness is "noticing what is going on inside me and around me" in this very moment with an open heart. Mindfulness is how I pay attention. It is a cognitive process not dependent on any belief or dogma. When I pay attention to my senses with friendliness and nonreactivity, I am practicing mindfulness. I experience mindfulness as a way to train in adding more peace and joy to my life. Coming back to mindful awareness gives me strength and solidity. It's not only a concept. It becomes the ground I stand on.

As my teacher Thay reminds me, "Mindfulness is always being mindful of something." You can mindfully fold laundry, paying attention to how the clothes feel in your hands—their color and texture—or to who made these clothes, who benefits from wearing them and from the care in your hands. You can fold laundry as an offering to your life and to your family, or you can fold laundry as a chore to power through. The open and nonjudgmental perception of mindfulness is an antidote to my conditioning. It allows me to be in the flow of life, giving and receiving.

For the last three and a half years, I've shared mindfulness professionally in a residential treatment center for teens. I work with a population that has depression, suicidal ideation and enaction, self-harm, body dysmorphia, addiction, ADD, ADHD, autism, and trauma. What I see most often running throughout all diagnoses is anxiety, eating disorders, and self-hatred—different manifestations of feeling not good enough or not worthy to be in the world. When I describe mindfulness to the kids I work with, I say we are going to pay attention to what is going on in us and around us with the essential ingredient of kindness or friendliness. We can notice what we are thinking and hate it and ourselves, or we can create some space and curiosity around our thoughts—as if we're looking at a friend's thoughts. Would we be so quick to condemn or judge a friend?

In my work, I've let go of my attachment to any prescribed form and the idea that one type of mindfulness is better than another—that the kids need to sit up to meditate, that focusing on the breath is a basic practice, and even that meditation or coming back to the body and mind is helpful at all. I've learned that my best gift to these kids, and to my own kids, is my stability. My presence.

The historical background of mindfulness is found in Buddhist texts. The teachings of the Buddha create a comprehensive system for understanding and living in harmony with oneself and the world. The birth of mindfulness specifically lies in the Buddhist teachings of non-preferential observation and meditation. Mindfulness is one facet of what is known as the Ennobling Eightfold Path—the list of instructions the Buddha gave for living a happy and compassionate life. Buddhism is one door through which it is possible to discover mindfulness: Buddhism always contains mindfulness, but mindfulness does not always contain Buddhism. It's like the difference between fresh water and ocean water. Both are water, but ocean water has salt: the added flavor of a wide-reaching path.

The Buddha uses two words to talk about mindfulness. The first is *sati*, translated as "remembering." The Buddha tells his disciples to remember their actions and words; in the Satipatthana Sutta, translated as the Four Foundations of Mindfulness, the Buddha points to four fundamental areas of awareness: the body, the feelings, the mind, and all mental states. The second word used in connection to mindfulness is *sampajañña*, which means "clear comprehension." The Buddha used this word when he told his followers to pay attention when they were getting dressed, standing, sitting, walking, and even using the toilet. Mindfulness contains both a remembering focus and an awareness of actions filled with clear comprehension.

Followers of the Buddha were encouraged to live their lives "ardent, alert, and mindful" and to put aside "greed and distress."

Making an effort to stay with awareness, free from distress, brings pleasure and friendliness. The Buddha was often depicted with a half-smile on his face when he meditated—no accident. Mindfulness is an integral part of the Buddhist path, and these are the teachings that protect me from making a hell realm of my life. When I step into mindfulness, I am inhabiting a specific present-moment attention described by the Buddha.

It's great to learn. I love learning, and it's easy for me to wander into the world of historical Buddhism—I love the details of who said what, who believes what, and the maze of discussion about historical accuracy. But intellectual learning can only take me so far. When suffering gets real, knowing which branch of Buddhism has six perfections and which has ten doesn't help me. It's a different matter for me to bring my mind back to my breath, back to my feet, and to calm myself when my child is in the ER. That's when conceptual knowledge becomes my bones in the present-moment application of mindfulness. In these moments I can rely on the training I've done, whether with ancient, traditional Buddhist practice or simply the countless times I've noticed the temperature of the steering wheel in my hand.

Learning something only to know it intellectually is like becoming an expert on onion soup recipes but never having the experience of cutting an onion. If I only learn, I remain separate, not doing the practice or getting into the messiness of peeling onion skins, tearing up as I chop. I never hear the sizzle of hot oil in the pot. I remain at an arm's length from my own life. Learning about mindfulness is an invitation to try it for yourself, to get in the kitchen and make the best mess you know how to make, knowing that you are doing this thing called meeting yourself in each moment. If I am only learning to sound smart to my Buddhist friends and I fall apart when there's a catastrophe, what's the point? I'd be better off learning about the stock market—I'd impress more people.

In My Life: Today, I have been on the Buddhist path for about eighteen years. In 2013, I was ordained in a Buddhist order as a lay (non-monastic) person. My early thinking has shifted: I've learned all

Buddhists aren't intolerant, angry people who believe this life is merely a dream and that the best way to salvation is to remove yourself from the unevolved messiness of it all. My experience with Buddhism has put me on a path to transform the largest obstacles in my life.

One of the first transformations came when I turned my attention to my inherited generational rage. Despite being wounded by rage and anger as a child, I found myself reenacting what I had tried so hard to avoid and spilling rage onto my own children. Each time I raged at my kids I was filled with shame and quickly apologized, but I didn't know how to stop. I was passing on what I had absorbed through watching and learning in the house I grew up in. I didn't know rage was an addiction, or that I got a hit of dopamine and endorphins when I screamed and blamed. One day, when Bella was seven, she said, "You always say you're sorry, but you still yell at us." She was right, and I realized I had the choice to either transform my anger or to transmit it to my own kids.

I'd been meeting for over a year with a local Plum Village Buddhist community called a *Sangha*. A Sangha is a group that studies the teachings of the Buddha, called the *Dharma*, and practices meditation and mindfulness together. The Plum Village tradition is the form of Buddhism that originated in a community located outside Bordeaux, France, where Zen master Thich Nhat Hanh settled after being exiled from Vietnam in 1966 for opposing the Vietnam War. Thich Nhat Hanh continues the lineage of Master Lin Chi, the patriarch of Vietnamese Zen, and adds a component of social engagement unique to the Plum Village tradition. This pro-social focus grew naturally out of Thich Nhat Hanh's formative monastic years spent creating social service programs to support the poor, rebuild villages, and advocate for peace during the Vietnam War.

Once a month in my Sangha, we read The Five Mindfulness Trainings. These trainings are the teachings that the Buddha gave his followers 2,600 years ago in the form of protective ethical precepts, updated by Thay and his monastic community to challenge and guide us to meet modern life with compassion and clarity.

After Bella told me the truth about my anger, I was struck by the Fourth Mindfulness Training on Loving Speech and Deep Listening:

When anger is manifesting in me, I am determined not to speak. I will practice mindful breathing and walking in order to recognize and to look deeply into my anger. I know that the roots of anger can be found in my wrong perceptions and lack of understanding of the suffering in myself and in the other person.

When I first heard these lines, they were utterly foreign to me. I didn't know people who did not speak when they were angry, and I had no idea what "looking deeply into my anger" meant, much less how to do it. I had been sitting and meditating with a Sangha and listening to Thay's talks for a year, and I had learned about caring for my feelings with mindful breathing and slow walking meditation. I was determined to make a change the next time I became angry.

Soon I was at home at the end of a long day. I was tired and cranky already, and the kids had made some mess I felt compelled to clean up. My feelings quickly snowballed into a solid mass of rage. I knew if I stayed in the house, I would start screaming. Feeling like someone else was controlling my body, I opened the door and walked outside into the cool nighttime air. It was dark and raining, and as I stood on the porch, the urge to turn around, walk back into the house, and explode at my kids flushed through my veins. I didn't think I could bear it for one more second. It felt like a restraint cutting into me, like I was tied to a chair, desperate to break free and do what I knew. But part of me remembered that I wanted to do something different.

I took a breath and moved my foot forward. *I can't*, I thought. Another voice inside me said, *One breath, one step.* There was burning in my body and mind as I breathed out and moved my other foot forward. I felt that fierce pull toward familiar rage and brought my mind back—*just this breath, just this step.* I continued to walk and breathe outside. After a while, I felt the rain on my cheeks. I realized I was standing in the dark, wet and alone, feeling something different than anger—it was calmness. I had no idea how long I had been outside. It could have been minutes, or an hour. What I did know was that I had made it to the other side of my rage. The anger was out of my body, out of my mind. What was there was hope. I had done it once; I could do it again.

That was the beginning of my trust in this path. That was how I first put this teaching to good use and how I worked to protect my kids from the painful inheritance of rage. Since then, I've found more and more wounds to transform, for myself and for my children. I took Thay's teachings into my heart and have found in him the greatest teacher of self-love I've encountered in my lifetime. Through his example, I have touched the truth of nonduality and learned that when I care for myself, I care for others. First as a daughter, then as a parent, I was educated to put others first; it's taken a while for me to see that taking care of myself is the best gift I can give to my kids.

Slow, mindful walking was one of the first practices I used to calm the body and mind, and it is one I continue to return to often. Deliberate slowness can provoke a physiological change in the body and mind, which function as one. I've returned countless times to my steps and breath when my daughter was in the ER, when I felt scared or helpless, and when I've felt unsteady waiting in airports, in train stations, or in malls. Mindful walking is a portable and accessible practice.

Mindful Walking

Mindful walking is a basic Buddhist practice of moving slowly with full awareness of our steps and contact points. With this technique of walking, attention is placed on the movement of the foot. The Forest Monks in Thailand call mindful walking *jongrom*, a Thai word that means to walk back and forth in a straight line. The practice is also called Walking the Dharma. In the Vietnamese Zen tradition, the word used is *kinhin*, a Japanese phrase that literally translates as "slow walking." Slow walking is an excellent way to be present with strong emotions like fear, anger, anxiety, or grief. When we experience these powerful emotional states, the body, mind, and attention can easily be carried away. In anger and fear, the nervous system releases a cascade of stress hormones, including adrenaline and cortisol, which cause wide-reaching reactions that occur in a nanosecond. The body gets ready to respond quickly in fight, flight, freeze, or tend and befriend mode.

Though fight or flight mode has made it into our common lexicon, tend and befriend is a newer term. In 1998, researcher Shelly Taylor found that female animals under threat move into a social, connective mode Taylor named "tend and befriend."[1] Prior to her research, studies included only males who demonstrated attacking, fleeing, or freezing responses to physical overwhelm. Unlike their mates, female animals are more likely to seek social support and bonding in response to a threat. This response is a way to preserve safety for dependent offspring. We can see these responses mirrored by human animals in social society, where women tend to focus on connecting and caretaking under stress.[2] The entire range of sympathetic nervous system responses are adaptive, creative ways humans are hardwired to respond to threats to keep themselves and their children safe.

Our minds and nervous systems work on a priority level. The first priority is always to stay alive—ask questions later. This means that any stressor, whether an email from work, a child with abdominal pain, or an expired car registration, triggers a threat response. For me, this activation can feel urgent, like I have to get out of the situation. It can be extremely uncomfortable. I notice adrenalin burning in my forearms, agitation, and anger. Sometimes, a rush of confusion and helplessness grinds me to a standstill. My heart tends to feel like it has grown twenty times bigger and taken over my stomach, and I may even lose my ability to speak. I've learned to pause when I notice these sensations. Instead of rushing into conflict or caretaking, hoping I can figure things out despite being so off-center, I intentionally slow down. My mind then gets a new signal: I am not under attack. Just as the mind informs the body, the body also informs the mind.

16

Slow movements can help move the body into a calmer state, whereas quick movements like running, hitting, fighting, and yelling keep the body running a circuit of panic, anger, fear, and reactivity.[3] Slowing down tells the mind "I am safe: everything is okay." When this message is received and my mind calms, I can find my wisdom again. I am not helpless; I can take my child with stomach pain to the emergency room. I can recall that I do know how to write an email with care, even if I need to express something difficult. I've experienced this shift as one of moving from intense irritation or fear to mental clarity.

Mindful walking allows the mind to settle and supports this clarity. Just as silt and dirt get churned into a pond by storms and movement, when the same pond is undisturbed, the silt and dirt settle, and still water allows a clear view of what is there. This is the effect of mindful walking. Thich Nhat Hanh recommends practicing mindful walking when we are calm and resourced so the practice becomes engrained for when we need it. It requires training to have the ability to recall and enact this practice when we are fully triggered. I tell the kids I work with, "When you're panicking, you aren't going to say, 'This is a good time to try something new; let me pull out this card of instructions I've been saving in my back pocket.' No; you lose your capacity to learn anything when you are activated. The mind doesn't take a chance on what it doesn't know when you're under threat." To access walking meditation during an event of anger and alarm, we need to have integrated this skill into our bones. When we are triggered, it is not the best time to try to introduce a new response; often, we lack the capacity to consider another strategy. The Greek philosopher Archilochus sums this up by saying that under duress, "We don't rise to the level of our expectations; we fall to the level of our training." We train for the race so we will be ready when it happens, and parenting, to me, is like an ultramarathon, not a sprint.

Recently, my teenage son came into the kitchen, where I was walking with slow steps. "Uh oh, what's wrong?"

"Insurance," I said, taking another step.

He nodded. He's used to me handling my frustration and anger this way.

Walking from the car to the grocery store, into work or the coffee shop, we are usually focused on the future. We plan what our day will be like, consider our coffee order or the work ahead of us. Leaning into the future, we sacrifice the moments of actually walking toward our imagined reality. We can use these seemingly inconsequential moments to continue to bring mindfulness and calm into our day. Walking mindfully, feeling our feet and steps as we make our way to the bathroom or the parking lot, we can stay aware of our bodies. We find that there are no wasted moments. With simple awareness of the body moving, we can show up for ourselves and develop calm and resilience continually in our everyday lives.

Acknowledging that we may travel and move around the world during our lifetime, Thich Nhat Hanh adds the reminder that we are fully home when we step into the present moment. This body is where we begin and end. It is our true home. With each mindful step, we have the opportunity to come home to ourselves and to our life. Our life is only available in this body, in this moment. Thay tells us that when we walk with the understanding that we are already home, we can stop running. We are sovereign over ourselves, and we are not pulled into the past or the future. When we come home to ourselves, we can stay strong in a storm. When we can walk mindfully as parents, we no longer lean into the future or the past; we straighten up and reclaim our lives in this moment. This moment is the one in which we can be useful to our children and to ourselves.

EXERCISE

Invitation to Practice Walking Meditation

---

1. Start by standing with your legs hip width apart. Breathing in, shift all your weight to one leg. Breathing out, shift the weight

to the other leg. As you continue shifting your weight with each breath, notice how it feels in your feet. Feel the ground beneath you. This is the intentionality you want to bring to walking.

2. Lift one foot slowly with attention, place it, and feel the earth as you step forward.

3. Lift the second foot at the same rate and step forward, feeling the earth.

4. When you've established a rhythm, start to add the breath. Breathe in as you lift, move, and place the left foot; breathe out as you lift, move, and place the right foot.

5. Keep bringing the mind back to sensation: the soles of the feet in contact with the earth and the movement of your body.

Expansion

Some people enjoy walking very slowly, noting the intention to lift the foot, the shift of weight, and the increasing feeling of contact as the foot bears the weight of the step. I like noticing the subtle moment when the weight placed on one foot transfers seamlessly to the other. The famous Forest Monk Ajahn Chah remarked that Westerners looked sad practicing such slow walking. He encouraged a more natural movement in which attention is focused while we move at our usual walking speed. If we have surplus energy or are feeling agitated, we can begin by walking briskly while focusing awareness on the sensation of the entire leg moving or on the subtleties of balance and flow present in the whole-body motion of walking. After a period of walking quickly, we may want to slow down as the body downshifts into a more mindful state.

We can practice mindful walking either indoors or outside. Walking indoors or in nature, we can enjoy walking not as a means to arrive, but as a moment in which we fully show up for this experience. Thich Nhat Hanh invites us to walk in nature with others and to enjoy the beauty around us and the support of our friends while we practice. When we walk outdoors, we can move at a pace that reflects our own sovereignty and remember we are part of the beauty of the living, breathing earth. Walking with mindful steps in nature, we can nourish ourselves both internally and externally as we receive the gifts of beauty and solidity from the earth.

Thich Nhat Hanh offers us *gathas*, a type of Zen poem, to recall our aspirations as we walk. These are words we can say to ourselves after we have linked our steps with our breathing. Stepping forward with the left foot we can say silently, "I have arrived." Exhaling and stepping with the right foot, we say, "I am home." Children can be taught the simple and profound gathas of "Yes" as they breathe in and step with the left foot and "Thanks" as they exhale and step with the right foot. The "yes" is a yes to life, an acceptance of the wonders of this cosmos, and the "thanks" offers gratitude for each breath and each moment, honoring this life in which we are heir to countless gifts of beauty, kindness, and connection.

Creating our own gathas allows us to find support by listening to our own hearts. I have often used the gatha "Walking on" (inhale, step) "the strong earth" (exhale, step) to remind me that I can access my own strength and solidity with each step, even if I feel helpless and hopeless. I can find solidity here, in this earth. This earth is my home; I am made of the earth, not separate from it. Using this gatha when I feel shaky or fragile, perhaps after getting frightening news about my kids or hearing of loss, reconnects me to my source and reminds me I have more resources than I can see right now.

Practicing regularly to increase capacity and solidity, in my experience, is not a dry and painful task. It has benefits beyond crisis preparation. It increases my ability to show up fully for all aspects of my life, including my relationships. It even helps me slow down and find joy I would have otherwise overlooked in my focus on getting things done and fixed. This is what I want to offer to my children and all children: my solidity, my capacity.

CHAPTER TWO

The Truth of Suffering

Now this, monks, is the noble truth of stress: Birth is stressful,
aging is stressful, death is stressful; sorrow, lamentation, pain,
distress, and despair are stressful; association with the unbeloved
is stressful, separation from the loved is stressful, not getting
what is wanted is stressful. In short, the five clinging aggregates
are stressful.

—*Dhammacakkappavattana Sutta: Setting the Wheel of
Dhamma in Motion*, TRANSLATED BY ṬHĀNISSARO BHIKKHU

In My Life: After taking care of my siblings growing up, I had no
illusions about the work of parenting. I did not want children. When I
was a teenager, staying home and taking care of the little ones felt like
a huge drag. In my twenties, armed with a metalsmithing degree, my
attention turned to building a jewelry and design business. There was
always more work than I could accomplish. I was tense and worked
sixteen-hour days. I wouldn't say I was happy, but I was passionate
about my craft and what I was making. I had responsibilities—show-
rooms, employees, and representatives. I believed my value was equal
to the amount of recognition and success I earned. This dependent
self-worth kept me running fast, trying to please as many buyers as
possible. I had high highs when there was a successful show and low
lows when my expectations went unmet. My happiness was tied to the
number of sales orders I received.

My business began to grow, but I was increasingly unfulfilled and unhappy. My days and evenings were taken over by work, planning, and managing employees. This wasn't the freedom I thought would come from owning my own business. I felt like I was working to pay everyone else with very little time left over for me. I hoped it would get better. I hired people to take on some of my duties, which created a different type of stress: Would they be as efficient as I would be? Would they try as hard as me? My life was running me. Over time, I became aware that I wanted something to change. I wanted more freedom and ease, but I didn't know how to get there.

My Jack Russell terrier, Pivo, came to work with me. He sat behind my chair and slept or barked protectively when the studio door opened. He came to the grocery store and waited in the car while I shopped. He slept in bed with me and my husband. He was my constant companion. One day, I told a friend who had a studio in the same building, "I wish Pivo could come into the grocery store with me, and I really want to teach him to talk." She gave me an amused look. "That's not a dog. That's a baby." I was shocked. I had spent so many years not wanting children that I hadn't recognized what was happening. I was in my early thirties, and in what I can only describe as biological insanity, every cell in my body wanted a child. And I did; I wanted a baby. I wanted a baby in the worst way.

After I recognized my longing for a talking dog as a veiled maternal desire, my husband and I started to try to get pregnant. I was sure, given my mother's track record with fertility, that it would happen instantly. No, not true. After a year of trying, we turned to science. Both my children were conceived in a doctor's office with the help of fertility drugs, hormone injections, and months and years of persistence, disappointment, and patience.

After the difficulty of getting the baby in came the unknown and frankly terrifying prospect of getting the baby out. There was no way it was not going to be painful. Knowing less drugs were better for the baby, I wanted to have a natural childbirth. I attended the Bradley Method natural childbirth classes. I had a midwife and a doula, recordings of soothing ocean waves, and even a birthing tub ready at the maternity ward. One night a few days past my due date, my water broke. *This is it*, I thought. *It's happening now.* The labor stopped and started, and I experienced a colossal backache known as back labor (where the baby's head is facing the wrong way). After two days, I was admitted to the hospital and induced. The baby's heart rate was erratic, spiking and dropping with the contractions. I developed a maternal fever, indicating that the baby was at risk for sepsis. The doctor stopped the Pitocin (the drug used to stimulate contractions) and told me, "You can have a C-section now, or an emergency one in an hour." I was beyond tired. "But I want to do this naturally," I said. This wasn't the way it was supposed to go.

"I have two patients," my doctor told me, and I realized then what having a child really meant. It wasn't just about me and what I wanted anymore; it was about my daughter and her life. The dream of an easy birth gone, my doctor performed a cesarean section and discovered the umbilical cord wrapped around my daughter's head. Her oxygen supply had been cut off during the contractions of the last two days. My first glimpse of my daughter revealed a silent baby with an unhappy face as she was whisked off to the neonatal intensive care unit (NICU).

Bella looked small and grim in the NICU; her eyes moved around the bright room, not resting on me. As I sat with her for the first time—perhaps it was the stiffness in her body or the searching movement of her eyes—I knew with certainty that this child would have suffering in her life. Only recently did I learn that babies who experience traumatic births can exhibit PTSD symptoms.[1] The best practice includes constant warm human presence to offset the fear response.[2] Under the bright light of the NICU, alone in her incubator with her arm strapped to a small board and an IV delivering antibiotics into her tiny vein, Bella had little reassuring human touch on her skin and no calming, ever-present mother to hold the ordeal of her life-threatening birth. Except for intermittent visits from me and family, she was left alone with her traumatic stress symptoms.

Four years later, in the same hospital, I had a second C-section. James was born with pneumonia and hardly any amniotic fluid, but he was a big, sturdy baby. Though he was in intensive care for ten days and on antibiotics to cure the pneumonia and help him breathe, when I held him there was a softness in his body. He was a calm baby who made eye contact, and during his stay in the NICU he smiled, a real smile. He had a full head of black hair with a small patch of silver on the side. He was a favorite of the nurses, who spiked his hair into a mohawk and dressed him in the cutest onesies they could find. From our first meeting, I felt that he had traveled this path before, and that with his mellow disposition, he would have ease and friendship in his life.

These two beings have been my teachers for over twenty years. My NICU impressions of them have been unfailingly accurate. My son has a calm, sweet demeanor, abundant friendships, and is very laid-back—sometimes too much so. The early trauma from my daughter's birth and temperament continues to unfold, often manifesting in fearfulness, anxiety, and social difficulty. Both of my children need me in different ways, and both have made me stretch and grow in ways I would rather have not. Parenting has taught me more about the truth of suffering and how to handle my suffering than any other job on the planet.

The Unavoidability of Dukkha

The truth and existence of suffering applies to all of us, and to you personally. Yes, you. You suffer, and I suffer, because life includes both pain and our response to experiencing pain. The word for awareness of suffering in the Pali language of the Buddhist scriptures is *dukkha*. The literal translation, from the prefix *du* (bad) and the word *kha* (hub of a wheel), is "bad hub of a wheel."[3] We've all had the annoying experience of the wonky shopping cart wheel—the subtle unsatisfactoriness or downright unwieldiness caused by a small shift in geometry that can create such an unhappy shopping experience. The precision of the Pali language offers a variety of dukkha flavors ranging from dissatisfaction to life-threatening terror. All are contained in dukkha: the hangnail and the tsunami.

This chapter's opening quotation is from the first teaching the Buddha gave after his enlightenment. In this teaching, he shared the insights of countless lifetimes of meditation and training, and he named all the circumstances of suffering or pain we will find in this world. Some of us are allergic to the word *suffering*. Scholar monk Ṭhānissaro Bhikkhu translates *dukkha* as "stress." If that is more useful, please mentally substitute *stress* where I use *suffering*. Suffering is seen as a teacher, something inherent in our lives that provides the opportunity to learn the ennobling way of power and strength. Merriam-Webster defines suffering as "to endure death, pain, or distress," and the definition of pain includes "emotional distress or suffering." Pain can be both mental and physical, and neuroscience shows us that all pain happens in the mind.

The underlying truth of the painful feeling of dukkha is found in any moment of perceived imperfection—moments when we want things to be different. A modern list from the Buddhist Publication Society includes both parenthood and childlessness, both hope and hopelessness, as states that cause stress or dukkha.[4] When things are hard with our kids, having children can be a source of suffering. If we are childless, seeing other families sharing closeness and belonging with their children can be a huge source of pain. Suffering is dependent on causes and conditions. Calling something painful or unsatisfactory is based on our circumstances, history, personal situation, and mind-state.

When Buddhists talk about suffering, they mean something very precise. Dukkha, or suffering, is divided into three general categories.[5] The first is the suffering of physical or psychological pain, our own or our child's (*dukkha dukkhata*).[6] The second is the suffering of the constant maintenance of the assemblages of existence and this thing we call a body (*sankhara dukkhata*)—think doctor and dentist appointments, the walls needing paint, the oil change, the never-ending tasks that keep life running. Third is the suffering of constant change (*viparinama dukkhata*) that comes with knowing happiness and ease will not stay around forever.[7] Your child's team will not always win; their test scores will vary. Your kids will not always be happy or well. Buddhist nun Pema Chödrön sums up these different states of dukkha: "Suffering is inevitable for human beings as long as we believe that things last—that they don't disintegrate, that they can be counted on to satisfy our hunger for security."[8] Dukkha includes all assembled things that have no permanent, independent identity and cannot exist without lots of support in their creation and maintenance—in short, everything we see, touch, and are.

Thich Nhat Hanh uses the term *interbeing* to describe this truth of no permanent, independent identity. Looking deeply into my body, it is clear that my blood contains iron and sodium as well as calcium and potassium from the earth and that the water in my cells is as old as this planet. I can see how the shape of my body is the result of inherited DNA. The air I breathe was filtered by the pine tree outside; the strawberries in my breakfast contained photosynthesized sunlight that my body now uses as sugar and energy. When I step into this truth of interbeing, I see I am never alone or by myself. I am supported by the whole cosmos. The idea that I am a fixed solid self—I am my title, a personality type, or the sum of my liking and not liking—begins to dissolve when I drill down into what it means to be alive on this planet.

This is the teaching of *anatta*, or the understanding that there is no stable and permanent fixed self-identity. This can rock our world, as we are used to labels to define ourselves. A few months ago, I learned it was bad manners in France to ask someone what they did for a living when you meet them. In the United States, that's one of the first things we ask. If I meet Dora at a party, for example, some of the first questions I ask to show interest are, "What do you do for a living? Do you have kids? Where do you live?" These questions help me to categorize and to form a picture of Dora: white-looking, she pronouns, forty-something computer analyst living in Silicon Valley with an eighteen-month-old. This image of Dora ranks education level, race, income, gender, and stress level; creating such an image is a natural protective response to encountering an uncertain world. Our little selves are always trying to find out who is safe and who isn't. Who is like me and who is different. Who do I need to protect myself from? My internal vigilance always asks: *Is it safe to be my true self around you, without judgment?*

What would it be like if I met Dora and asked, "Who do you love the most in the world? What was your happiest childhood memory?" My picture of Dora would include some biographical information about her, but I'd also know her as someone who loves, someone who can feel happy, and someone who comes with an ancestry instead of merely as someone who is a job, a degree, and a label. I would see her as a living process lacking a fixed identity, not a product.

Anatta is contained in Thich Nhat Hanh's concept of interbeing. This is the understanding that we are made of everything in this world. We are full of ingredients, inherited genetics, and the lives of our ancestors—their habits and struggles, their traumas, strengths, and fears. We are shaped and conditioned by these lives even if we did not know the people who came before us. Our lives are supported by the air we breathe, the water we drink, and the food we eat. When we consider all the supporting conditions that bring us into existence, we see that what we thought was a separate, reified self is actually a container for everything in this cosmos. Thich Nhat Hanh reminds us that we are empty of a separate self, but full of everything else.

Living in relationship means we are going to experience things not going to plan. These bodies become sick; our children may make choices that threaten their safety. I would love a magic talisman that would keep the people I care about safe and well, that would ensure my kids were always protected and make good decisions. This natural desire is at the heart of suffering. My daughter may take risks with her life or date someone who drives recklessly. Even though I may dislike what is happening and clearly see the pain of the situation, on a very basic level this suffering is the unfolding of natural consequences. This happens because that happens. It's okay to suffer. Suffering happens. All beings suffer. I will suffer, and my kids will suffer. If I am at home with the idea of impermanence, aware that bodies and mind-states don't last, I have less fear and resistance when I encounter difficulties. This, in turn, can make space for the possibility of handling my suffering in a different way—with compassion.

When we are in the middle of suffering, awareness of its unavoidable nature can help us stop fighting against the natural course of events. It can take the sting out of suffering to realize that each person on this planet will encounter pain and suffering in their lifetime—it is not personal, and there are no quotas. In difficult moments, I often tell myself, "Suffering feels like this. It's okay to suffer. Everyone suffers." Putting my suffering into perspective and linking it to a universal feeling calms me and releases the tension of disapproval. If your child is unwell, you are suffering. It is okay to suffer. Knowing we are suffering means we are called to respond. Although we cannot control the experience of psychological and bodily pain, we can undo a layer of protection and resistance when we let go of the notion that suffering and pain are wrong. We can learn how to take good care of our suffering.

The Meaning of Suffering

In Buddhism, suffering is viewed as the necessary grit that polishes our rough edges smooth. Rather than something to avoid, suffering, when understood correctly, can actually lead us to great freedom. Thich Nhat Hanh has given entire retreats about the goodness of suffering and the ways in which it creates the beautiful qualities of compassion, wisdom, and kindness. Many people have heard his saying, "No mud, no lotus."[9] In his Dharma talks, Thay often tells us that just as the most beautiful lotuses grow in the deepest mud, so our suffering is needed to transform our unwholesome qualities into flowers. If we never suffered, we would not understand the pain of another and would be incapable of compassion.

When I lean my hand against a hot stove, thermal receptors send pain signals through my spinal column and ultimately to the area of my cerebral cortex responsible for processing sensations in my hand.[10]

It's almost as if my mind has a small model of my body and it jabs pins into where there's a pain point. If my child has disordered eating and is binging and purging and obsessively checking their body, I will feel pain too. This pain runs the same circuitry in my brain, but there is no exact physical location for my mind to put a pin in. I can't bandage my sad heart. This pain is invisible, but it is just as real as the burn on my palm.

Parenting a child who is in distress can make parents feel like everything they do is wrong. Like they didn't get the training needed to save this kid, or there's some essential parenting skill they are lacking. In spiritual circles you may have heard the saying, "Pain is unavoidable, but suffering is optional." This doesn't mean that when we are suffering, we are to blame. It is an invitation to check in. The distinction between suffering and pain that helped me to understand my role in my own suffering without blame or shame came from Sharon Salzberg.

I was sitting a seven-day Loving Kindness retreat in Barre, Massachusetts. That's the term, *sitting*, because this retreat included lots of sitting meditation. A year before, I'd had surgery on my right hip to repair a torn labrum. As my right side healed, my left labrum said, "I give up," and tore. So, while I could now move freely on my right side, I was limping on my left. I had always meditated sitting on a cushion on the floor, and I had the opinion that the real stuff of meditation only happened on a cushion. On day two of the retreat, my back hurt, my left leg refused to lie down quietly and rest, and I couldn't relax or concentrate. I had so many blankets and cushions supporting me it looked like I was having a tag sale on my mat.

I moved into a chair. I didn't want to sit in a chair. The Buddha never sat in a chair. How could I get to blissful one-pointed concentration sitting in a bougie chair? Then my back started hurting in a new and different way. I used blankets, cushions, and tried leveraging my seat forward with cushions under my feet and arms. Nothing helped. Still determined, I sat. And I sat. With my legs hanging down and blood pooling in my feet, I started to worry I would get an embolism and end up like the woman who flew from Australia to London and died when she got off the plane. It was all wrong. Sharon Salzberg, who sat in a chair, asked our group, "What are you adding to the experience?"

My added extras included missing my pre-injury body, planning my medical interventions, disliking all the props I was using to try to bring some ease into this new postsurgical body, and believing what I was doing was not okay. This form of sitting was not okay; there was something better. The truth was, I was going to be uncomfortable. That's it. I was going to have a physically uncomfortable experience, and all the other stuff I was adding—my judgment, dissatisfaction, and squirming to get away from discomfort—was the suffering. Thich Nhat Hanh says, "Don't amplify the pain." Sometimes things are painful; sometimes they suck. The more I come to terms with what I am adding to a given circumstance (turning up the volume of my pain by comparing, for example, or by pointing out the unfairness, or guilting or shaming myself), the more I learn how to stop making myself suffer.

My Dharma teacher, Joanne Friday, used to say, "If I see that my suffering is dissatisfaction, I can recognize that it's a choice." Learning to see this truth, I can increase my ability to accept the conditions of my life and my child's life. It bears repeating: accepting suffering is not a passive state in which I throw up my hands and give in. Accepting suffering is what needs to happen for me to take wise action. If I accept that my child is sick, I can take him to the doctor; I can do something. Getting familiar with suffering is the way to understand how to end suffering. This is in no way an invitation to relish suffering or to feel guilt or shame when we do not like suffering. Of course we don't like it! Of course we really don't like it; of course we don't want those we love to suffer. We aren't supposed to. Suffering is a powerful message that we need to attune to our internal state and to our surroundings.

All teachings can be used to help and support us, or they can do violence and punish. We are not bad practitioners or parents when we react with fear and anger to our own suffering and the suffering of our children. Much violence is done to ourselves and our relationships when we judge what a good person, a good Buddhist, or a good parent would do in this situation.

If our lives are all consumed with suffering, we lose our joy and become useless to care for ourselves and those around us. We become part of the suffering, and we can sink into the ocean of despair. Nourishing our joy and happiness can seem impossible (and even wrong) if our child is in distress. It may seem selfish to think of what is still positive in our life. But when we remember suffering is part of life, not the whole, we have more resilience. And yes, happiness is possible, even when so much is wrong, out of our control, and unwanted.

Nurturing joy is crucial for maintaining our stability and compassion in challenging situations. We need this balance, this joy on the other side of the scale, to give us the ground to hold our suffering. My teacher Thay reminds us, "Don't ignore your suffering, but don't forget to enjoy the wonders of life—for your sake and for the benefit of many beings."

Parenting and Suffering

All phases of parenting involve understanding where we stop and where our child begins: What is ours to care for? What is beyond our control? Parenting a child whose life and well-being we cannot control can bring huge suffering. This is part of being a parent and caring for a vulnerable life outside ourselves. In doing so, our love and concern doubles our availability to feel suffering.

My friend, who is a member of the same Buddhist tradition I practice in, had a four-week-old baby. He texted me that the baby's blood work had come back "out of range for metabolism," and that things were difficult right now. We spoke on the phone, and he said, "There's this toxic positivity where I keep saying it's going to be all right. If I say it enough, it's true."

"This is suffering," I told him. "When you're in the ER with a newborn, that is not a wonderful moment. Some moments suck. This is suffering, and it's okay to feel the suffering. It doesn't have to be silver-lined or somehow okay."

"I think that's the part that's been missing," he said in a quieter voice. "I didn't want to admit I'm suffering."

If we don't understand the uses of suffering, painful moments are more painful and awful because they feel worthless. What makes suffering valuable is what we can do with it. When we accompany ourselves in suffering, our ability to care for our feelings makes the moment wonderful. This moment is an opportunity for us to be a compassionate presence for ourselves. First, though, we must recognize that we are suffering and that we are worthy of our own compassion.

A common misperception is that life is *just* suffering all the time. What a depressing thought. What I've learned in my lifetime is that there is never just one thing: the mud and the lotus are constantly there. Sometimes the flower of the lotus is so small I can't see it, and it looks like all I have is mud. But then, slowly, a bud forms, and I get a peek at one or two petals. Some days I even get the flower, open and vibrant, the gift of loving life. Even on days of beautiful blooming the mud is also there, supporting the flower, but I see it differently because I am also experiencing the flower. The mud is what gives it roots and makes it a lotus. I need to notice how the mud and the lotus are different to understand what's happening in me. I need to know when I am in pain and when I am not, to see that both happen together, often quite subtly. When we recognize suffering, we also recognize that the opposite is here too. Thich Nhat Hanh reminds us that suffering and happiness *inter-are*. Our joy is made out of the material of suffering.

When I see how interconnected I am with my children, I have the opportunity to access more joy and happiness. Sometimes it feels like having children opens us up to more suffering, but it's not only one way. Having children stretches our hearts to include more suffering *and* more joy. Life holds both. Our children's lives hold both as well.

Parenting is fertile ground for examining suffering. In 2005, a meta-analysis synthesized data collected in the late 1980s by the US National Survey of Families and Households. Analyzing responses from over thirteen thousand adults, researchers found parents consistently had more depression than equally situated nonparents. Parents with small children had the highest levels of depression, but no type of parent reported less depression than nonparents. Depression is the experience of helplessness and hopelessness—the sense that we are powerless to meet the conditions of our life. In depression, we believe we have no choice. This belief is suffering.[11] Although these findings use data from over three decades ago, I wonder if anything has changed. We are starting to see the collective effects of COVID-19 and the marks of formative years defined by distancing; we haven't yet seen the full impact of these years of isolation, division, and virtual, screen-only relationships. It seems as though there's more suffering to come for both children and their parents.

We know, either from being parented or from parenting, that raising a child is hard work. Some days, months, and years are beyond hard and can even feel unbearable. As painful and unwanted as circumstances can be, this is our journey and teaching—and theirs as well. When we witness suffering in someone we love, we don't know the outcome, what will be lost or gained. We may not welcome or seek to prolong the experience, but we know suffering has causes and roots, some of which we may never see. Awareness of the reasons for suffering, even reasons we cannot see or trace, can help us release some of the tension around the injustice of suffering. Steamrolling over the suffering to get to the bright side or the insight disavows empathy, the place where two hearts and minds meet and the one in difficulty feels held.

This empathy has been crucial in allowing me to recognize the suffering in myself and others. Finding an empathic connection with our children without losing our footing and falling into a pit of despair and shared pain is possible. Accepting the reality of suffering is not an invitation to become passive and defeated. Just the way parents recognize that a child is sick and seek medical help, recognizing suffering gives us a choice; now we can do something about it. When we know what causes suffering, we know how to release from suffering. Like a child who learns not to put their finger into an electrical socket, we too can learn how not to choose the circuit that amps up our suffering.

Being on a spiritual path is not about being perfect. To my knowledge, pursuing a life forever safe from mistakes or conflicts has not proved to be a successful strategy for enlightenment. Holiness recognizes our own undimmable birthright of goodness. Holiness is about being fully responsible for our own thoughts, feelings, words, and deeds, and, as Mother Theresa said, about remembering that we belong to each other.

In My Life: In October 2014 my son was eleven and in middle school, and I was at his last soccer game of the season. I don't recall the score, but in the last play of the game, a teammate kicked the ball at close range to my son. He was hit in the right orbital socket and temple and blacked out. "Yeah, it's a concussion," the trainer told me as we looked at James's dilated pupils. I noticed his skin was red and raised in hives, and his body was shaking. "He'll be fine in three days."

That night, James's head hurt beyond his ability to stay calm, and we ended up in the ER. An MRI told us there was no brain bleed and no chance of stroke. "Give it time; let him rest," and he would recover, they said. But three days came and went without improvement, then a week, then two. James was not getting better; his head hurt continually. He couldn't tolerate lights and he had nystagmus, where one eye moves independently of the other. We sought specialists and therapy. James went to vestibular therapy for his neck and eyes, physical therapy to help him reconnect with his body, and vision therapy for eye exercises, concussion assessment, and cognitive testing. We visited a pediatric neurologist, who put him on antinausea and migraine drugs. Neither relieved his symptoms.

Luckily, I could put my projects on hold. I drove James all over Connecticut to appointments and hounded him to do his exercises. He couldn't read or look at screens. He was behind in his schoolwork, and after a few weeks, I didn't know how he would catch up. After a month, I wondered if he would repeat the grade. Most difficult were the friends who didn't visit, all the kids who were too busy to stop over or call, and the loneliness I saw in my son as he became more and more isolated.

That same fall my daughter, Bella, began her sophomore year of high school. She had begged us to attend a boarding high school. Despite apprehensions, my husband and I supported her choice. We hoped it would give her more social confidence to be away from home and living with a group of kids. Toward the end of her freshman year, Bella had begun to complain that she was depressed. She saw the school counselor, whom she disliked. We took her to two other therapists, hoping she would talk to them. Bella rejected each one and refused to talk during the sessions, even when we insisted. By the end of freshman year, she had become increasingly withdrawn. She ate ramen noodles alone in her dormitory and refused to go to the cafeteria. She didn't participate in school life and shut herself in her room to watch Netflix when she wasn't in class.

We hoped sophomore year would be different. Bella had been adamant about attending this particular school—she'd worked hard to get accepted, felt she "belonged there," and wouldn't consider going anywhere else. A month into her sophomore year, Bella told me with hesitation that she was depressed and starting to fantasize about killing herself as a way to end the pain of not belonging. My spouse and I set up an intervention with the counseling staff at the school. Despite Bella's resistance, she agreed to be assessed for depression. The psychologist who tested her told us Bella's depression scores were in the ninety-eighth percentile—she was "one of the most depressed students" he had ever seen. These were not the high scores and superlatives a parent dreams of.

Since Bella was so resistant to support, my husband and I decided that home and parental supervision would best combat her isolation and help her to get the treatment she needed. In October 2014, two weeks before my son's last soccer game, we pulled Bella out of school and took her home. Within a week she began at another high school, enrolling mid-semester and with no friends. Bella's social anxiety made meeting people difficult, and she raged at us for taking her out of the school where she thought she should belong but had been so unhappy. Every day it was a struggle to get her out the door. She sobbed when she came home and blamed us for her loneliness. "Why did you take me out of school? I hate it here!" She was inconsolable. I desperately tried to get her an appointment with a psychiatrist, but the wait was a month or longer. Finally, Bella began seeing a doctor and received medication; I had some hope that she would improve.

A week after starting medication, Bella began threatening suicide and told me she was stockpiling pills. I searched her room and couldn't find anything. We hid the Tylenol and Advil. Now she looked at us with hatred and anger. She didn't cry anymore, but openly screamed, "I am going to kill myself to make this stop. I hate my life; it will never change!" My stomach hurt so constantly that I kept thinking I was coming down with a virus. I was so focused on Bella's pain that I couldn't see the stress in myself. I was caught in an unwinnable situation, trying to help someone who doesn't want help. At the same time, I had a daughter who wanted to end her life and a son who couldn't live his life the way he wanted. I felt powerless and constantly worried. I woke each morning with the immovable heaviness of dread. Before I opened my bedroom door I would steady myself in case this was the morning I found Bella overdosed or dead.

One of my most difficult moments was the recognition of how burdened and exhausted I felt. There was so much distress in our lives that I began to imagine that if Bella did take her life, at least the intensity of that pain would end. This thought opened another level of suffering; I now felt guilt and shame over my inability to bear it all without complaint. I wondered where that maternal unconditional love I was supposed to have had gone. The thought that my child's suicide would end an inescapable hell was chilling; I dared say so out loud to only one friend, who could hear me without judgment. I had exceeded my capacity to be with suffering.

Since then, I've learned that to be with suffering, I need to understand my relationship to it. The Buddhist understanding of suffering is different than that of the mainstream world. In the mainstream world, we are encouraged to believe that modern science and human advancements are so mighty, they can guarantee the life we think we are entitled to: a life free from pain and suffering. We are encouraged to believe pain and suffering are unnatural. If we do the right thing, the smart thing, we are promised a life of abundant health, youth, and happiness. We can outmaneuver suffering and pain. It took me years to realize that even if I did all the things the child experts told me, nurtured my children's bodies and minds and heroically engineered a life to keep them from harm, I could never wipe out suffering permanently.

We are all searching for the code that will allow us to live beautiful, satisfying, Pinterest-worthy lives free of sadness and grief. If there is a sickness that lingers or a depression that resists treatment, not only is it wrong, but somehow, we're at fault. If we were holy enough or evolved enough, we wouldn't suffer, and if we were doing things right, the ones we care for wouldn't either. There is an unspoken conviction that if you suffer, and those you love suffer, you have failed.

The Four Noble Truths Apply to You Too

I am not the first parent who wanted to protect their kids from pain. The historical legend of the Buddha shares the extreme efforts his father made to shield his son from suffering, keeping him behind the compound walls of their palace where life was manicured and everyone was healthy and happy. It wasn't until the Buddha escaped into the world that he encountered the Four Heavenly Messengers—an old man, a sick man, a corpse, and an ascetic—and gained true insight into the nature of suffering. These four messengers are credited with opening the mind of the Buddha to the path that allows us to know both suffering and the way out of it. The last messenger the Buddha encountered, the ascetic, was a holy man who was able to live peacefully amid the inescapable pain and challenges of life.

Understanding not only that there is suffering but also that there is a way out of suffering is the basic message of Buddhism. The Buddha is recorded as saying, "I teach only one thing: suffering and the end of suffering." He didn't say I teach two things; when we know the reasons for suffering, we can see that there is another road we can take that leads to a different destination. When we see the roots of our suffering, we see the roots of our liberation. The Four Noble Truths are the Buddhist basis for understanding how suffering works in the world. These truths are:

1. Suffering (dukkha) exists.
2. There are causes of suffering: *samudaya*.
3. There is a way out of suffering: *nirodha*.
4. The Ennobling Eightfold Path (*magga*) is the road map out of suffering.

This is what the Buddha first taught after his enlightenment. The Four Noble Truths contain all the virtue and wisdom of the Dharma, the path of practice.[12] The First Noble Truth is *dukkha sacca*, the truth of suffering.[13] This is the realistic understanding of vulnerability—life contains suffering, and all suffering asks to be understood. All suffering is dependent on causes and conditions. Despite the vicissitudes of life that threaten our own and our children's existence daily, we don't often acknowledge suffering. As parents, we can see many causes and conditions that lead to suffering in this unpredictable world of pandemics, natural disasters, and just plain irritations. Born into fleshly forms, we are subject to old age, sickness, and death. We tend to be more comfortable contemplating these changing states for ourselves and our parents than for our children.

Our search for safety and ease in an unpredictable world leads to the Second Noble Truth: there are reasons for suffering. Thich Nhat Hanh calls this truth the "path to suffering."[14] Just as all beings need food to continue, so does suffering. The Second Noble Truth asks us to consider how we are creating and feeding our suffering and the suffering of our children. This requires looking deeply.

The roots of our suffering are inside ourselves, driven by a ceaseless craving called *tanha*, or thirst. This is the craving that wants more money, food, or fame; what you have will never be enough, despite it being all you will need in this lifetime. Tanha is a thirst that will never be satisfied.

This grasping shows up as painful mental states called the *kilesas* (defilements), or the three poisons. These poisons are the basis of harmful behavior in the world: ignorance, delusion, or confusion; greed or desire; and hatred, aversion, anger, or violence.[15] Ignorance is not pathological evil or badness. Ignorance is the mistaken belief in separation rather than interconnection, in the duality of the self and other. The Buddha would call this "wrong view."

At the bottom of this wrong view is a misunderstanding of our impermanent and interconnected role on this planet. Seeing ourselves as an independent, fixed, small self creates the often-unconscious habit of participating in strategies of hatred, violence, greed, and privilege. We believe that doing so will mean getting more for ourselves and our group and that this will keep us safe. We see this played out in our burning planet, in the oppression and enslavement of others, and in our aversion to acknowledging our contributions to systems of domination. As a parent, I may want my kids to be safe and well while being less concerned about the children halfway around the world. My beloved is more important than the unknown, the unloved.

Knowing and understanding suffering, we are able to consider the end of suffering. This is the Third Noble Truth: there is a way out of suffering. The Pali word for this is nirodha. *Rodha* means "prison," and *ni* means "no." Once we know what is causing our suffering, we can do something about it. We can get out of jail. When I see that holding my hand over the flame is causing me pain, I can move my hand.

Abandoning the cause of suffering is not easy, especially if I think doing so will endanger me or my children. We need guidance and support to do hard things. The Buddha gave a set of instructions for finding the way out of suffering. The Fourth Noble Truth, called magga, states that a path of liberation leads to *nibbana* (*nirvana*). Nirvana means the cooling of the flames or the extinguishing of the ceaseless thirst of tanha. The Buddha described nirvana as the end of stress. The path of liberation is known as the Eightfold Path out of suffering or stress and has eight areas of focus: right view, right intention, right speech, right action, right livelihood, right effort, right mindfulness, and right concentration.[16]

Thich Nhat Hanh points out that all eight categories are contained in every one, and every one is contained in all eight.[17]

Because all facets of the Eightfold Path lead to liberation from suffering, the Fourth Noble Truth can look like a conversation. When we practice right speech—speech that includes kindness and appropriate timing, considers usefulness, and comes from a loving and true desire for connection, for example—we live in accordance with all the other path factors such as right intention and right effort, and we protect both ourselves and those we interact with from harm.

If I want a better relationship with my child, looking into my words and my intentions behind the words may lead me to stop beginning my sentences with, "If you ever want to be on your own, you're going to need to ..." (work when you don't want to, clean up after yourself, take accountability, and so on). Maybe I'd consider whether this sentence contains kind words; is it useful, and does it land in a way that helps my child to see what is important and that I want what's best for them? Or does it distance them from me? Do I invite eye rolls, feelings of shame, or sound judgy? Living in accordance with the Eightfold Noble Path means I might choose instead to say, "I want you to learn life skills so you can be independent, and it's important to me to live in a clean house right now. Would you be willing to sweep up after dinner tonight? And if not, can we talk about what's going to work for both of us?"

Such an approach reflects a life in alignment with truthfulness and sincerity. By respecting my child, giving them clear instructions, and making space to hear their view without punishment or blame, I am practicing in accordance with path factors such as right view. In doing so, I recognize my needs as well as theirs. As parents, anything we do has an impact. When we model living with care for ourselves, for our children, for the earth, and for all beings, we send a powerful message deeper than words. We teach what we live.

The Buddha told his followers, "I teach what is possible. I do not teach anything that is not possible." His words are encouragement; we too can take the path out of hell to something better. This is enacting The Four Noble Truths: seeing our suffering and knowing how to accompany it.

When we stop reacting and step into recognition and care, we can attune to what it feels like when the suffering ends. This sustained compassion and awareness is living the path of liberation. This is the experience of joy, a step on the path.

In My Life: When my kids were little, we visited a relative in a gated community in Florida. It was an upscale place with landscaped swaths of New Guinea impatiens in orange and fuchsia. There was a guard who waited for personal approval from my relative before allowing our car beyond the entrance. Everywhere I looked was pristine and sang the song of money and privilege.

Taking a solo swim one afternoon, I met an older woman in the pool. When I told her I taught mindfulness and was Buddhist, she got a distant look on her face and asked me if I thought people with money suffered. I could see her bracing herself as she waited for my answer. I looked at her for a moment before replying, "Rich people suffer. They look better doing it, dress better and drive better cars, but they still suffer." As she listened, her shoulders released and her face relaxed. My answer soothed something in her that was longing to be acknowledged—even those who seem to have everything will encounter pain and suffering. Having money didn't disqualify her from receiving compassion. Money doesn't protect us; in fact, it can bring more suffering, and running after it can separate us from our children.

I grew up on the poor end of a rich town and encountered firsthand the shame that having less can bring, especially when you are surrounded by those who seem to effortlessly have all the things you want. The clothes I wore came from paper bags in the church basement. I hoped no one would recognize their old castoffs; I told the lunch ladies my name and got checked off the list of kids who couldn't pay full price for lunch. Being different, and especially different with less, was suffering. And still, I know there were kids who saw my circumstances with adequate heat, clothing, and food as wildly luxurious. No matter where you are on the financial continuum or the privilege scale, no matter how much you have or don't have—we will all encounter suffering in our lives. We all have unique personal suffering.

Looking at our own suffering invites a larger perspective. I recall how painful it was to hear a family member dismiss my suffering as "first world problems." My problems are real in my life, in the world I live in; they are my particular and unique suffering. At the same time, awareness of suffering helps me to own my privilege and see myself in a larger, universal context. I know that people living in black and brown bodies face daily aggressions and that I, living in a white body, do not share that collective suffering. I am aware that there is vast inequality in education and generational wealth. I know that the country I live in has committed and continues to commit violence and sustained racism, that white-centering happens again and again, and that the gender nonconforming among us face aggression and othering on a systemic level. Yet I also know that when there is a child in crisis, parents—no matter their race, their background, or their financial status—suffer. At work I see kids of many colors, genders, and sexualities, each with their own unique suffering, and each one a source of suffering for their folks. If we disavow our suffering, on the individual or collective level, we learn to abandon ourselves, to cover over and cover up.

The Buddha's Five Remembrances

To get more familiar and comfortable with our own suffering, the Buddha taught the Five Remembrances. In the Upajjhatthana Sutta, the Buddha recommended that people of all genders, both house-holders and monastics, reflect on five truths. These truths are facts that we will encounter because we live in bodies and love other beings. Reflecting on these truths is not designed to create pain and bring despair, but to wake us up to the inescapable transience and impermanence of life.

These remembrances help us to recognize what we have right now and to celebrate the love and connections available to us in the present moment. These reminders softly shine a light on what is often a tender place we are afraid to look at. When we learn to stay with the universality of these truths, we see that change and separation are not just for us and our children, but for everyone who is born. Aging, sickness, and death are not personal.

EXERCISE

Invitation to Practice the Five Remembrances

I had a copy of these truths taped to my bathroom mirror for years to read each time I brushed my teeth. You may like to keep these words nearby so you can read them as a daily practice:

"I am of the nature to grow old. There is no way to escape growing old.

"I am of the nature to have ill health. There is no way to escape ill health.

"I am of the nature to die. There is no way to escape death.

"All that is dear to me and everyone I love are of the nature to change. There is no way to escape being separated from them.

"My actions are my only true belongings. I cannot escape the consequences of my actions. My actions are the ground upon which I stand."[18]

When I read these to a friend, thinking of being separated from her children brought her to tears. These remembrances aren't to torment us, but to prepare us and to wake us up to reality. Every time I read these words, I am reminded to tell the people I love how they enrich my life; I do not wait, because I do not know the future. I am also reminded that my actions are all I own and all that is guaranteed to follow me. What I do can make a difference. I can show up and care deeply for myself and others. Reading the Five Remembrances can help us return to our heart's desire to embody compassion and presence.

CHAPTER THREE

Not Abandoning

We should not be afraid of suffering. We should be afraid of
only one thing and that is not knowing how to deal with our
suffering. Handling our suffering is an art. If we know how to
suffer, we suffer much less, and we're no longer afraid of being
overwhelmed by the suffering inside. The energy of mindfulness
helps us recognize, acknowledge, and embrace the presence of
the suffering, which can already bring some calm and relief.

—THICH NHAT HANH, *The Art of Living:*
Peace and Freedom in the Here and Now

In My Life: It was the December of 2014 that was so hard. A month
after my husband and I had pulled my daughter from boarding school in
her sophomore year and enrolled her in a local high school, she told me
she was hiding pills to take. "I hate this school," she told us daily. When
I encouraged her to give it some time and suggested that things would
change, she snapped back, "Nothing is going to get any better. It's always
going to be bad." I searched in her room and looked under the mattress,
in the backs of drawers, but I came up with nothing. I locked up the
family's Tylenol, Advil, and Benadryl. I was scared for my daughter, and
also for my son, who still had severe concussion symptoms six weeks after
being hit with a soccer ball.

It was around dinnertime at our house in Middlebury, and Bella
was lying on the couch in the family room. I was standing at the kitchen

44

island when I heard her say, "I took sleeping pills," her voice like a little girl's, "I'm starting to feel weird." I put her into my car and began to drive. As we got closer to the hospital I began to wail and cry, not holding back my terror and anguish. Bella was admitted and put in observation. I practiced mindful slow walking in the hallway of the hospital, breathing in as I took one step and breathing out as I took the next, the same way I did to overcome my rage. Focusing on my breath and steps helped me stay present instead of getting lost far in the future.

Bella hadn't taken enough medicine to do permanent harm, but it was enough to scare her, me, and my husband. My daughter was fifteen and in the hospital—parental authority allowed me to commit her to the adolescent psychiatric unit, which I did. For the first time, I felt I had real support for her. As much as my spouse wanted to be there for her and for me, we were both stretched thin: between caring for James, extricating Bella from her boarding school, enrolling her in another high school, finding a psychiatrist for her, shuttling her to school and therapy, keeping up with my son's treatments for his concussion, and keeping private all of this for fear of folks judging all of us, we had little capacity left. We didn't know how to keep Bella safe, and we didn't have the individual support we needed to be there for each other. We just kept going; we couldn't stop. We were living in a hell realm with no rest.

But in the hospital, there was real help. "Go home and get some rest," the on-duty nurse told me. "She's in the safest place." It was true. Bella was in a room with only a gurney and a surveillance camera. In adjacent rooms I saw two older women held in beds with restraints, shouting "Help!" and sounds that didn't make words.

"Don't leave me," Bella screamed as I walked out of the small holding area. I walked away feeling numb, exhausted, and like a terrible mom for leaving. Driving home, I knew she could not hurt herself where she was. That month, my husband stopped working. We split child-care duties and divided my son's medical and therapeutic appointments. We visited Bella in the hospital. She mostly stared at us and blamed us for committing her. She was angry and "one of the most resistant," according to the hospital psychiatrist. She wasn't making progress and refused to cooperate. My son's concussion was not improving, and the pediatric neurologist couldn't explain why his eyes didn't track together and his head still hurt. I had no idea if he could go back to sixth grade or would miss a year of school or more. Each day felt like a punishment, like simply more hours to get through. I wanted to make time speed up, to find a moment in the future when both kids were healthy and able to care for themselves.

We Want Safety

The world can feel like one big threatening ball of danger and create well-reasoned fear and vigilance. Every living thing is born wanting to be safe. Swiss-born Buddhist teacher and psychotherapist Akincano Marc Weber tells us that the basis for happiness is what does not kill us.[1] Survival is the ingredient for rudimentary happiness—finding conditions that maintain our lives.

At our most primitive, we have much in common with simple life-forms. Even single-celled organisms will move toward sugars and away from acids. We are born into vulnerable bodies that often live in environments where seasonal temperatures can kill us. Inherently, humans have a powerful, protective threat-detection system. Our limbic, emotional center is a marvelous interconnected system that has done an admirable job of keeping the human species alive. The unreserved greed of human industry means that in some regions, drinking the water can kill us. The food we eat can give us diabetes, heart conditions, obesity, and can kill us. Our jobs cause stress and hypertension, which, yes, can kill us. The downside of constant vigilance is an often-exhausting state of arousal and worry that makes us raw and sensitive. As stimulation increases, we can become more and more tense, fearful, and anxious. Taking on responsibility for a helpless being like a child can add another layer to our struggle for safety. My friend with the four-week-old baby reflected this in a text he sent me: "This is so stressful. We've already been to the ER, and I can't protect her from the world."

A facet of tanha—the unquenchable thirst, craving, or hunger that is the root of suffering—is the desire for more, better, best for ourselves and our children. This desire can show up as anxiety and manifest as an over-stuffed schedule for us and our children; so often, we expect superlatives and achievement. This wanting mind is constantly dissatisfied; there's always something sweeter and better to cover the taste of what is bitter and painful. This conviction is an inheritance of the human condition and stems from the delusion that we are not supposed to suffer. It is a misunderstanding that is reinforced daily in our culture. We are taught from an early age that happiness is a reward and suffering is a punishment; if we do everything right, neither we nor our children will suffer.

As someone raised in American consumer culture, I have received hundreds of thousands of messages through advertising, media, and societal modeling that instructed me to care for difficult emotions with consumption. When I feel afraid or anxious, I can eat or drink something to take the edge off. If I am sad or mourning, I can buy new things—retail therapy. I can exercise, gamble, play video games, take drugs, eat, watch TV, self-harm, or have sex to avoid my feelings of loneliness, boredom, or helplessness. Rather than offering true safety, these activities end up making me more afraid to be alone with these difficult parts of my life. I get better at hiding, and if I practice these avoidant strategies for decades, I get very good at abandoning myself. I become disconnected from myself, my feelings, and my life.

Where does safety come from? I feel safe around those I trust. Developing trust takes time. I learn over time if someone shows up and does what they say they will. I trust friends who can be there. I don't trust those who are absent or try to change the topic when I share something hard. If I never check in with myself and don't show up for myself when things are painful, what kind of friend am I? I earn my own trust through showing up and being willing to stay present with myself, no matter what is happening. This trust is nurtured each time I turn toward my suffering with compassion and curiosity. When we give ourselves conscious permission to experience safety and solidity despite external conditions, we help calm the nervous system and break the continuous grip of fear and reactivity.

If we have a long history of retreating from our distress, we may not have the ability to stay with ourselves for very long at first. We may need to practice feeling safe in our bodies by beginning with one or two breaths of presence and gently extending the territory of our capacity over time. By practicing stopping and pausing, we train our ability to support and comfort ourselves. This is a practice, however, that cannot be rushed or forced into ripeness. Be gentle. It can take time to learn to trust that we can support ourselves when we need it.

The Buddha directed his followers, "Be islands unto yourselves. Be your own refuge."[2] This refuge is a place of solidity and strength that we all possess, though it may be obscured by worry and doubt about our children's well-being. We cannot be centered and balanced if we are afraid. If we are afraid, our kids feel it. As you read this, take a moment to simply notice the amount of tension or relaxation in the body. Ask yourself, do I feel safe right now? If you are a single parent called on to perform the heroics of providing for your children and offering emotional support alone, it is easy to feel vigilance and fear. If you are a person of color experiencing the implicit bias of white-dominated culture, aware that a black or brown-skinned body is perceived as a threat by many white folks and institutions, you may be yearning more deeply than words can express to experience safety and belonging, for yourself and for your children.

We know the body and mind are one and that we cannot have a calm and tranquil mind in a wired and tense body. Conversely, it's impossible to have a relaxed body when we are furious, despairing, or panicked about our children. When we begin by calming the body, the mind understands that we are not under threat and begins to release, soften, and let go of protections. This allows us to have greater ability to think, reason, and respond to what's unfolding for our child. Bringing your awareness to the breath and resting in the wisdom of the body, which knows exactly how to breathe, can be a bridge between calming body and mind.

Vedana: The Three States of Human Experience

If you doubt that you have the habit of retreating from suffering, try noticing hedonic feeling tone, or *vedana*.[3] Vedana describes the pleasant, unpleasant, or neutral feeling tones of our visceral reactions to experience. These reactions are not considered—you don't need time or thought to discern the pleasing from the painful. All our feelings, the whole range of our emotional life, can be divided into these three categories: we like, we don't like, or we don't notice. These responses are instantaneous and reflect what our bodily senses find attractive, repulsive, or too subtle to register. Vedana is present when we wrinkle our nose at the sour smell of spoiled milk or lean into the scent of a lilac. There is vedana when we initially don't notice the sound of the faraway lawn mower but then find ourselves annoyed as it gets closer.

Vedana also includes a natural movement away from what is painful and toward what is pleasant. Meditation teacher Joseph Goldstein writes, "Almost all movements are an attempt to alleviate some kind of pain or discomfort."[4] Is this true? If we pay attention, are we leaning away from the unpleasant, or the idea that something will be disagreeable, and toward something more enjoyable?

Developing awareness of how fluid and reactive the mind is begins by observing the constant wanting and not wanting reactions present in every situation or thought.[5] This requires deep listening to an internal voice that often operates below our level of consciousness. We may not be aware of a thought or reaction until we notice something is wrong or, more often than not, there is *someone* who is wronging me. When we become aware of the subtle push and pull of wanting and not wanting in our daily lives, we can start to move toward a nonjudgmental, compassionate acceptance of ourselves. We can understand that these vulnerable bodies and hearts just want to keep their kids and families safe from pain.[6] We can hold our reactivity, our fear, our anxiety, and our irritation with an attitude of empathetic care and be willing to comfort ourselves, no matter what.

Self-Reflection

The ability to tolerate our own discomfort requires paying attention to our moment-to-moment experience. This may not be possible in crisis situations in which the urgent need to respond to what is happening around us may have fatal consequences. It is useful to practice tolerance and paying attention to get to know our reactivity before we are in a crisis. When we can learn in lower-stakes circumstances that our emotional content comes and goes—even the really big stuff—we have more solidity and aren't thrown off-center as easily in more challenging circumstances.

When we look at how the mind moves even when we are busy with tasks, there is always the subtle movement of vedana. As we attune to this relentless push and pull, we become accustomed to our signals and desires and can notice how quickly they come and go. When we unveil the constant flickering of wanting, we can stop taking our desires so seriously. When we stop responding automatically to signals of unrest and rejection, we gain the freedom to be with what is.

EXERCISE

Invitation to Practice Awareness of Vedana

One way to develop this awareness is to set a timer and check in. Take a day where you will be able to make some notes at fifteen- or thirty-minute intervals.

1. When the timer goes off, take a moment to check in with your body and your thoughts.
2. Write down the time and then your condition. Note if this moment is pleasant, unpleasant, or neither. Your journal may look like this: "12:00, My hair is wet from the rain—not wanting,

unpleasant. 12:25, I am alone in the library—wanting, pleasant. 12:40, Hungry. What am I going to eat? Wanting, pleasant."

3. Reflection questions: review the list of your day, noting the wanting, not wanting, and neutral sensations. Do you notice any reoccurring thoughts and reactions? Has anything shifted in the intensity of wanting or not wanting? When you notice and stay with a given feeling tone, does anything change?

The Dalai Lama shares the benefits of practicing observing emotions and thoughts without reacting: "You will not fall into extreme states of mind: you will not get over-excited or depressed."[7] In addition, reflecting on the basic sameness of the human experience—all beings, just like me, desire to be free from pain and suffering—is a simple way to develop acceptance of our shared human experience.[8]

Many people use the word *acceptance.* The word *accept* in common usage has a tinge of passivity to it, but *acceptance* is linked to possibilities. Acceptance is the first step to understanding, compassion, and wise action. Acceptance allows me to parent the child I do have, instead of the one I'd like to have—the imaginary one with greater self-control, maturity, and perspective. When I don't accept my child as they are, I add to my own frustration and increase the tension between what is and what I believe would be good enough. Acceptance means I get to do something about the relationship and situation I am living in instead of being distracted by the circumstances I'd like to be in.

This does not mean what is happening is always wonderful and we should unquestioningly embrace everything in and around us. We practice nonreactive awareness to see behind our automatic responses and break the spell of being jerked from one emotion to another. When we pause and look with calm eyes, we can recognize the truth of our reality. Accepting what is does not mean we stop, powerless to create change; we can take steps to remove the cause of our pain. Just as we change our behavior when we see it causes suffering, we can stop doing what causes us to suffer.

In My Life: Since I grew up with a Catholic mother who adhered to Vatican laws, it was no premarital sex, no birth control. Girls, cover up! By the time I was eight, I knew we did not talk about sex, relationships, gender, or even attractions in my house. Thinking you were pretty or beautiful was vanity, and that was a sin.

As my daughter, Bella, approached the age of dating and sexuality, I noticed flashes of annoyance whenever she revealed intimate dating details about herself or her friends. *Why is she telling me this?* I'd think. Then, another part of me would wonder, *Why am I reacting like this? I should be glad I know what's going on.* I had spasms of frustration when I saw Bella going out in tiny T-shirts that didn't reach her navel, and often, I'd ask her to change or put on another shirt. I knew her friends were wearing the same clothes and that even if Bella left the house in one outfit, there were no guarantees she wouldn't be wearing a different one twenty minutes later. Still, it was discomforting for me that my daughter was showing skin I believed should be covered.

My discomfort came from a war between my past and my future. Part of me wanted to shut out sexuality and sensuality, to parent the way I was parented, and part of me wanted something different, something freer and more accepting for my daughter. This unpleasant vedana was confusing until I realized: my uneasiness every time my daughter left the house showing off her belly button piercing or talked to me about who was doing what with whom came from wondering how this would look to my mother. I wanted my mother to think I was being a good mother. The problem was, I wasn't seeing my daughter in this. I was parenting my child in the shadow of my own parents. It felt like a radical act of rebellion to decide I wanted my daughter to feel good about her body, to be unafraid of her sexuality, and to be able to cherish herself.

What does it mean to you to parent for yourself and not for your parents or anyone else? Put down this book and ask yourself, "What are the best gifts I can give to my child?" Is there anything blocking your willingness to offer that? Is anything in you asking for your own care and understanding?

Recognizing and Allowing Our Emotions

To support our children and recognize their difficulties, we must first be willing to courageously look at our own emotional landscape. Feelings are natural ways the body and mind call for our attention and care. Feelings want to be understood. Many of us—especially if we are women—were taught to put our emotions, needs, and well-being far behind the needs of our children and others. Yet we create more suffering, for ourselves and others, when we attempt to outstrip our capacity for powering through difficult emotions. Akincano Marc Weber reminds us that, "Just because your needs are overwhelming doesn't mean my needs do not exist."[9] Parents may have trouble acknowledging that we have needs when our kids are in pain, but we do—especially in a crisis. This suppression of our needs does violence to ourselves. The radical permission to include all parts of ourselves—fear, happiness, anger, and terror—is an aspect of equanimity. Accepting what is arising in ourselves without condemnation or censure is the work of healing into wholeness and returning to love and care.

Many years ago, I had a spiritual teacher whose child committed suicide as an adult, in his late twenties. When she spoke about it, there was an ease and acceptance that I found baffling. She said his life, as abbreviated as it was, was "complete." Why wasn't she more distraught and grief stricken? She explained that her son had battled bipolar illness. His life and hers had been loaded with suffering related to his uncontrollable psychosis, which often turned violent. She had dealt with her own frustration, despair, and anger until she ultimately released her son from her expectations and desires. She exhibited a deep understanding that her son's life was his own. He had suffered enough, and although she loved him and missed him, she accepted his action. I had never encountered something like this before.

I saw the same level of understanding in a co-practitioner, a mother with a drug-addicted son. Her heart broke over and over as her son came through a succession of rehab visits, got clean, and then began to use again. She struggled with anger and blame and tried everything to save him. Her final decision to love and accept him just as he was without any hope he would ever change allowed her to move closer to him and to offer support, even when his addiction ended his life.

In the *Dart Sutta*, the Buddha talks about the practitioner who feels the real pain of being hit by a dart without adding blame and worry; he feels only the pain of this one dart. Someone who has not trained in acceptance, on the other hand, "having been touched by that painful feeling, he resists (and resents) it. Then in him who so resists (and resents) that painful feeling, an underlying tendency of resistance against that painful feeling comes to underlie (his mind)."[10] The person who refuses to accept the reality of their pain or heaps regret, anger, worry, and resentment on the already painful situation is like a person who has been hit with a second dart on top of the first. The pain of a child in distress is our first dart; how do we add or avoid the second? We all can handle so much. We make our jobs harder when we fight against what is. We have very good reasons for feeling as we do. We don't need to add blame and shame on top of pain.

Joanne Friday uses the Buddha's example to gauge our capacity to be with suffering. Though a teaspoon of salt added to a cup of water makes the water undrinkable, a teaspoon of salt added to a lake is undetectable. She says, "Some days I am a river, some days I am a teacup." If we can honestly look at our capacity moment to moment, we can see what we need to care for in ourselves. Do we need kindness or some understanding? Are we lost in pain and reactivity? Can we stop and consider what support we would like—community, ease, or space to mourn broken dreams? No part of us, no emotion or thought, is too terrible for us to look at with kind eyes and to hold with gentleness.

Noticing the Shape of a Painful Emotion

This is a meditation I have used with clients when emotions feel too big, as if they are going to overwhelm us. This practice can offer the experience of decoupling from the emotion and aligning ourselves with our bigger mind, with our source of compassion, so we can stay centered when we encounter strong emotions. This is a more advanced practice that requires the ability to slow down and check in with our emotional selves; it is inspired by Thich Nhat Hanh and the work of Dr. Richard Schwartz, the founder of Internal Family Systems.

Let yourself know that for this meditation you will be in charge of yourself, and you will only go as far as is comfortable. There will be no forcing, no "should" or "have to." This practice is about gentleness and accompaniment.

EXERCISE

Invitation to Practice with Painful Emotions

---

1. Calm and center the body.
2. Open to what emotion is arising.
3. Notice the shape, color, and contour of the emotion. Is it moving or still? Where is it in the body? Does it have a texture, a feeling, or an image? An age or a gender? Is it hot or cool? Does it change? Observe with curiosity and openness.
4. Find the outer edges of this emotion in the body. Bring softness just to the very edge of it, as if you are stroking a small bird.
5. Breathe and stay here, caring for the emotion. When your heart feels open, hold the emotion in your arms or on your lap.
6. Invite the emotion to breathe with you, teaching it to rest on the breath.
7. Ask the emotion if it has a beneficial message. What does it want me to know? What is it afraid will happen if it doesn't do its job?
8. Let the emotion know you understand. Thank the emotion for taking such good care of you, and invite it to rest now, in your care.
9. How does the emotion respond to this empathy? Make a plan so the emotion knows you will return to take care of it when it needs you.

10. Celebrate that you were able to show up for this emotion with care and capability.

Expansion

Begin by inviting yourself to rest in a comfortable, supported position. The eyes can be closed or softly focused on something that is restful. Return to your anchor of choice—breath, sound, or bodily contact—and let yourself rest in this safe and comforting place for a few minutes. When you feel a willingness to investigate, bring your awareness to the emotions arising in you. There is no rush. Let things unfold without forcing. Remember that your compassionate wholeness and stability is here, supporting you. As you encounter an emotion, allow it to arise before you while you stay solid. From this place of calm and stability, see if you can notice the emotion's shape and color. Do you feel it in the body? Locate it. Is it in the chest, sinuses, or belly? Does it pulse and move, tingle or clench? How does it express itself? Locate the edge of the feeling; find its shape. What color is it? Is it flickering or steady? Does it fill up the entire body, or does it perhaps settle on the shoulders and the back of the neck? Wherever the emotion is in the body, bring awareness to the outer edge of its shape.

Use your mind like a gentle caress to stroke the outer contour of this emotion. Our compassionate heart can let this feeling know that we see it and want to take care of its pain. It has good reason for being here and, like everything that arises, it belongs. Without trying to shift, eradicate, or judge, let your caring touch encircle the entire edge of this feeling like a warm cloak. Check how you feel toward this emotion. How does the emotion feel, being recognized and cared for in this way? If you notice resentment or dislike, come back to the anchor of breath or just sitting in awareness and restabilize until there is willingness to find out more about the feeling.

If your heart is open to caring for this emotion, offer to hold it in your arms or on your lap. This is an opportunity to teach this emotion how to breathe with you. Breathing together, acknowledge the beneficial intention of this emotion and how long this feeling has been working to keep you or your child safe, to care for and protect you. Whatever you've learned about the emotion's intention, give recognition and gratitude to this feeling, and let it rest in your arms, in your care.

Celebrate that you were able to be with this emotion without having it overwhelm you. Let the emotion know you will visit again. The more you can do this practice, the more you will strengthen your relationship with your emotional self and learn to trust that you can meet yourself in all moments.

CHAPTER FOUR

The Eight Worldly Winds

Gain/loss, status/disgrace, censure/praise, pleasure/pain:

these conditions among human beings are inconstant, impermanent, subject to change.

Knowing this, the wise person, mindful, ponders these changing conditions.

Desirable things don't charm the mind, undesirable ones bring no resistance.

—*Lokavipatti Sutta: The Failings of the World*,
TRANSLATED BY ṬHĀNISSARO BHIKKHU

We want life to be filled with happiness for ourselves and our children. But life does not flow in one direction, full only of pleasant and joyful moments. In the Lokavipatti Sutta, the Buddha taught his disciples about the Eight Worldly Winds (*lokadhamma*), or Eight Vicissitudes, the changing states of the world that blow us around—sometimes to our delight, and sometimes to our dismay.[1] The Buddha told his followers that all our lived experience fits into these eight categories: *gain/loss, status/disgrace, censure/praise, and pleasure/pain*. All people, parents, and children encounter these eight changing states over and over in a single lifetime. The Buddha highlights how fickle these winds are and encourages his followers to see them come and go without falling in love with the good and rebelling against what hurts.

Sometimes we experience loss, and sometimes people will think the worst of us or judge our kids and, by proxy, our parenting. The knowledge that these states are temporary is, in my experience, not synonymous with acceptance, especially when it comes to parenting. Taking the long view and recognizing that all things change is a process. Knowing nothing lasts forever does not prevent us from wanting only the good stuff. We want our kids to be healthy and devoted to us forever, to stay away from drugs and alcohol, and to consider the future when they act. As a species, we are reluctant to accept the unwelcome truth that living in this world means we will touch each of the Eight Worldly Winds.

Marshall Rosenberg, father of three and founder of Nonviolent Communication, said the definition of hell is believing there is such a thing as a good parent. The world makes assessments; the same action will always elicit both praise and blame. To some folks, writing about my child's mental health will be shocking and seen as very bad parenting. Recognizing that whatever I do will be loved by some and hated by others was a frightening prospect. Especially with my background, I was afraid to be around disapproval. But gradually, I realized it wasn't the disapproval or anger that causes me pain, but my own reaction to it—my fear and running from it. Knowing this, I was freer to live honestly without being scared for my safety. As my mentor, Jori Manske, told me, "If I want to be perfect for everyone else, I have to live inside their judgments. To be perfect for myself means I live inside my own judgments." This helped me see that if I held onto the idea of perfection and believed *any* judgment, even my own, was the truth, I would suffer.

One of the most precious gifts we possess is the ability to choose where we place our minds. This truth offers us the possibility of standing solidly, firmly present and with compassion for ourselves, regardless of what the world is throwing at us—liking or disliking, good health or illness, an easy time or a major struggle. We may become hardened and embittered by our situation, or we may choose to find a subtle joy in our intention to befriend ourselves no matter what. We have the choice to react by raging against the injustices we or our children are handed, or to choose to touch our courage and remind ourselves that all states and conditions will arise and pass away.

The Buddha offers the image of a mountain to remind us of unshakable calm, even in a storm. Meditating on the image of a mountain is one of the most beloved meditations for equanimity and reminds us of our mountain nature, our own ability to stay solid and stable despite the vicissitudes of life. Thich Nhat Hanh offers us the visualization of the mountain in ourselves. *Breathing in, I touch the mountain in myself. Breathing out, I am solid.* We can sit like a mountain, not swayed by storms or worldly winds.

Pain Is Natural

Pain, destabilization, loss, reprimands, and people thinking badly of us can be some of the most unpleasant aspects of life. They are some of the most difficult moments to tolerate, for ourselves and especially for our kids. As humans, we have a natural aversion to these painful states. We create elaborate protections and arrange our lives to ward off the embarrassment, shame, fear, anger, and physical pain we are afraid of. But living in a body guarantees us pain—sometimes lots of it.

There is a belief that pain, injury, illness, losing one's health, losing money, experiencing discomfort, loneliness, confusion, frustration, or disappointment means something is wrong. If we have an illness like arthritis, diabetes, heart disease, mental health issues, or something chronic, it's an imposition. If these conditions are present in our children, it's worse. Disease and pain are not seen as integral parts of the human condition, despite the fact that 69.6 percent of women and 65.4 percent of men enrolled in Medicare (over the age of sixty-five) in the United States have two or more chronic illnesses.[2] The Western world and its access to medicine and technology gives us the illusory promise of an existence free from pain, discomfort, and suffering. Our relentless media exposes us to a stream of positive and happy images designed to stimulate the consumption of products that purportedly deliver fulfillment and even love and intimacy. While a home security system and a safe car may be desirable things, they can't protect us from life's fluctuations, nor can they assuage the disappointment, fear, anger, and frustration that accompany pain, loss, bad press, and blame.

Our societal conditioning trains us to disavow loss, disgrace, corrections, and all manner of pain and to move as quickly away from those states as possible. These states are doubly painful for parents, since there is a tacit belief that if we or our children are in pain or experiencing loss, we've contributed to it. We didn't exercise enough, eat well, or follow society's script. If we had read more self-help books, been more vigilant or careful, neither we nor our children would now be ashamed or embarrassed. We have been raised to view the myth of "happily ever after" as an attainable state.

The basis of balance or equanimity is understanding that below the constant surging tide of lows and highs beyond our control is a current of stillness within us. This stillness is our ability to stay balanced and strong despite the winds that shake us and our children. This nascent ability is here—we don't have to sprout it from a seed. It already exists. When mistaken beliefs of what is permissible and acceptable recede, our natural equanimity can shine with wisdom and patience on our lives.

Impermanence: Noticing the Changing World

The idea of impermanence (*anicca*) is one that we would rather not look at too closely, since it means that all my relationships and my life itself have a beginning, a middle, and an end. What's more, there is no website that tells me if I am nearing the finish line or simply cresting the hill of midlife. Buddhism is an experiential path. When we touch and experience anicca, it becomes the reality we see in all moments. While we can intellectually understand concepts, in our practice we are asked to do more than that. We are invited to integrate these truths into our beings and into every cell of our bodies until we are unsurprised by what is surprising. Because all moments are impermanent, change is possible in each moment.

I found out recently that the Pali canon records the Buddha teaching on anicca over one hundred times. The word we translate often as "impermanence" has a slightly different flavor in Pali, the language of the Buddhist scriptures. The root word is *nicca,* which scholar monk Ṭhānissaro Bhikkhu translates as "constant" and "dependable." The prefix *a* is used to indicate the opposite, thus anicca means "inconstant" or "undependable." These words contain the seeds of judgment; *dependable* or *undependable* are evaluations, and not simple observation. The word *undependable* is linked to the experience of frustration and disappointment that we don't necessarily associate with something breaking because it's worn out. The etymology of the word *anicca* reflects the truth that it is usually frustrating and unwanted when our children encounter suffering in their lives.

It's easy to get caught in the pleasant moments and to forget they are part of the pendulum of life. Just as there are days when we make all the green lights and no one we love tells us we are selfish or inconsiderate, there will invariably be days when we have nothing but traffic and no one is delighted with our best efforts. When we touch the truth—all moments, all highs and lows are just an edited snapshot of the full experience of life and not the whole—we can release clinging to the belief that things must be a certain way for us to feel okay. Can we consider the possibility of offering ourselves understanding and acceptance even when things are not going well, even when the people we love are having difficulty?

When we are riding the high water of the pleasant, the moments of connection and delight, we are taught that that's how life should be—these easy and sweet moments are our birthright and belong to us fair and square. Our children are supposed to love us. We are supposed to love them. We all get along. This is what the script says. The truth of life is that these moments of ease and happiness are impermanent. Their nature is to change; even the pleasant is unsatisfactory—it is made of unstable conditions.

Speaking for my species, we don't find impermanence comforting or comfortable. We want some firm ground—people who never change and consistent experiences we can rely on. We crave stability, belonging, and safety, but what we get are these vulnerable, fleshy bodies that disappoint us, need constant maintenance and protection, and, at some point, stop working altogether. Indeed, skin cells only last three days; the liver completely regenerates in about a year. Change is a hard thing to depend on because nothing is exempt. The future is never as we imagined it. If we limit our acceptance to times when those we love are healthy and well, when people love us and approve of what we do, we have given away our ability to create lasting happiness independent of external conditions.

The well-being of our children depends on so many conditions: if we have enough support, their level of health and immunity, their social situation, if they have people they trust, if they are being bullied—the list goes on. Each child is so different; we may have the experience of doing the same thing, only to have it loved by one child and criticized by another. Telling our children we care about them may mean we receive a hug and hear an "I love you," or it could mean we are left listening to a door slam followed by silence. Here, too, we see the Eight Worldly Winds at work: our words, actions, and appearance will bring us praise from some and blame from others.

At the end of his life, the last words of the Buddha are recorded as, "All compounded things are subject to vanish. Strive with earnestness!"[3] Everything is made of other things; nothing is a fixed, solid entity. Elements come together; our bodies are knitted from many cells. At the end of our lives, the body we are in breaks apart and becomes something else. A lily bud in a vase with time, water, and sunlight becomes a blooming flower. This phenomenon we call a flower also changes with time. The petals turn from white to brown; they wither even though we keep adding water to the vase and put the flower in the same sunshine that helped the bud grow. Gradually, the flower becomes something else. We stop calling it a flower—now it is a piece of compost or garbage. My body is the same.

This world lives with demarcation lines: this was my childhood, spent in this house with these friends, and then this is where I lived as a young adult with these interests and friends before I became a mother living in a new town with growing children. In this narrative, each portion of my life is packaged into a manageable chunk, each separated from the others by location and time. But there is no separation the day we stop being a child or the day we turn twenty-one; there is no separate life when we get married or widowed. We create mental compartments of a self, often based on time and place, but if we look at our lives, we see they unfold against a fluid and inconstant backdrop.

This is the truth of anicca, of impermanence. We believe we are a solid self—an ever-evolving being, separate and distinct, who lives independently—but if we ask our cells to confirm this truth, the cells just laugh at the notion of remaining one thing for a lifetime. They know they come and go. They can become cancer cells or a tree. My cells understand this truth much more gracefully than I do.

Witnessing change and the moment-to-moment shift of living is a central part of the Buddhist path. All beings, from the smallest single-celled animal to a complex human, will encounter the inescapable truth of impermanence. If we are honest about impermanence, we understand that everything we see—the house, the car, folks in a hurry to get to work, all the infrastructure, our family, and everything that meets our eyes—is subject to change and decay. It's all going away—even us.

Impermanence is not personal and can sound like a tremendous bummer, but this understanding is a way out of the suffering that comes from being attached to a chimera. I remember telling my Dharma teacher once during a pause in family drama, "Not much is going on; it's really quiet." She laughed and said, "Enjoy it, because it will change." Not surprisingly, she was right. When I forget that all beings and all conditions are impermanent, I set myself up to suffer. This craving for life to be predictable and dependable is directly tied to suffering, or dukkha.

It is challenging to think of people with the same understanding of impermanence and interbeing. When we look with our Dharma eyes, we see that we aren't the solid citizens we think we are; we are transient phenomena inhabiting the temporary construct of this society, and even this earth. The Buddha recognized that his teachings here on earth are subject to change and dissolution. There is nothing that will not change. Dukkha, anicca, and anatta (dissatisfaction or suffering, impermanence, and nonself) are considered the three marks of existence in the Buddhist worldview; they are the three truths shared by all. These three conditions are basic truths of living in these bodies that we cannot control, woven into a system that constantly falls into and out of balance. Everything keeps changing. It will shake you up, and it's not personal. As parents, we experience shock and disappointment when things fall apart over and over. Our children's lives aren't predictable. Impermanence makes no exceptions.

Susan's Story

Susan gives us an example of parenting with love and trust, even in the face of fear. Working as a nurse specializing in palliative care, her job brought her in contact with those in chronic pain approaching the end of life. This unique personal experience gave her a larger perspective on suffering and supported nonfear in the face of life's vicissitudes.

Susan was always close to her son Max. She appreciated his curiosity and drive to understand the complexities of mechanics. In high school, Max filled notebooks with drawings of cars and was fascinated by the engineering of water systems. Both Max and Susan experienced pleasure, praise, and good reputation when Max was accepted into the only college he wanted to attend and received an academic scholarship. This pleasantness, however, was not permanent. Susan remembers Max's freshman year: "He lost his way, and he drank a lot. He did not do well academically. His grades slipped." In fact, Max's grades fell so much, he lost his scholarship.

In his sophomore year, Max continued to have difficulty. He became depressed and, unknown to his mother, began to self-harm in an attempt to bear his own pain. Susan describes the night Max was taken to the emergency room: "I got a call, but he was over eighteen, so they wouldn't tell us why he'd been admitted." Max had cut himself, seriously enough to be taken to the hospital. "I was shocked he didn't tell me what was going on. He had to talk to a psychiatrist. That was a really bad night." The current of Susan's life shifted, and she found herself experiencing unwanted aspects of life's vicissitudes in the form of multiple losses and deep pain, not only related to her son, but also to her parents and extended family.

"My partner's mother was dying of lung cancer. When she died four months later, my own mom was in hospice. It was hard on my son. My mom had a cancer recurrence, and I was trying to help her get through treatments. My focus was related to the pain of this—she had several crises and ended up in the hospital, all while I was working full-time. It was a very anxious time."

Susan's training as a nurse gave her the skills to be present for her mother during her illness and death. Her wealth of contact with dozens of families rocked by suffering and loss increased Susan's ability to understand the fluidity of change. She knew that all lives are touched by sorrow. Though she was deeply concerned for both her mother and her son, Susan's intentions included maintaining a calm, loving presence. "I didn't feel panicked because I felt that these are difficult phases. It's my son's life; we can't make choices for him, and we can't control what he does. I knew he would come through."

In his junior year, Max made a connection at school. "He was in a program that gave him opportunities to work in a business and feel accomplished," Susan reflects. "He really blossomed again after he got into his major. He graduated and began working right away." As I write this, Max is recently married and working at a job he loves. Both his and Susan's lives currently contain pleasure, gain, praise, and good reputation, all the pleasantness of the Eight Worldly Winds. While these are not fixed states, they are lovely moments when we have them. The tricky part is to enjoy them without clinging to them, steady in the knowledge that life is made of many unseen influences and that pain belongs.

Causes and Conditions

No matter how I believe life should go, each individual's life unfolds because of generations of causes and conditions, seen and unseen. Although there may be pain and unhappiness, it is not purely mine to control. This doesn't mean I don't try to make life better for myself and those I love. It means I give up the all-or-nothing thinking that says I cannot be happy unless everyone is traveling in the direction I want.

This is how we open to life: we start with a willingness to include one thing, and then we include what's next. Like ripples in a pond growing wider and wider, we open ourselves to meeting our lives in an ever-widening range of experience until our presence becomes like the surface of the pond responding to a breeze. This is what we are called to do: to respond with care to this moment, to what's next, and to all lives entire, with no part left out.

You will never meet anyone who has only approval, gain, success, and fame in their life. Just as our lives contain all elements, so too do our children's. They will have pain, loss, blame, and disapproval. Their lives are made of innumerable causes and conditions that we cannot glimpse. We cannot shield them from the vicissitudes that flutter through the world and through their lives, no matter how painful this truth may be. At best, we accompany our children with a fierce determination to titrate suffering and an acceptance of the limitations of our desires and abilities. Meditation teacher and psychotherapist Tara Brach speaks about "taking our hands off the wheel" and allowing ourselves to meet the conditions of life.[4] We don't have to struggle to turn the wheel in our own direction because, in truth, we can't.

For some of us, acknowledging what is really going on can feel impossible—it's too big, and we may feel powerless to eradicate the cause or change the situation. When we see the pain of another, we may react with anger because we can't tolerate our own powerlessness. We may tell our child they are ungrateful for our efforts or minimize or dismiss their problem because if we listen and understand, we would touch a pain beyond our control. Perhaps we would rather turn away, assign blame, or see ourselves as the innocent victim who inherited this suffering without cause. These responses can become a habit. Our perception of injustice and the reaction of anger protect us from having to try and from risking loving and losing.

Thai Forest Monk Ajahn Sumedho uses the phrase "This is the way it is" to look at emotions and mind-states without judging.[5] This simple phrase is the groundwork of acceptance. It is a renunciation of efforts to make things go our way, and it contains patience with our reality. But mostly, it offers space to see that the way things are is not personal. When we can pry ourselves away from our emotional response to our child's experience and interject care and understanding between ourselves and the struggle, we can begin to look with curiosity and tolerance.

I've often found myself twisting with a painful emotion, wondering how to make it go away most quickly and cure this pain. When I recognize that this discomfort, which feels like it's in the way, is actually the very thing I need to be with, I can say, *This is what confusion feels like…. Oh, there's a tension in my rib cage; there's agitation in the skin cells of my arms. Oh, this is knowing confusion.* While the sensation may still feel unpleasant, my steadiness grows from my willingness to stay with what is arising.

When I stop and uncouple from an emotion, I can better fulfill my intention to show up as a friend to myself, recognizing that what is arising is not about me. The world isn't doing something to me. When I do this practice over and over, through small and large upsets—and with pleasant emotions as well—I fill a reservoir of trust. *So this is what joy feels like, and happiness*—these too are opportunities to care for all our experiences. This not-abandoning brings solidity and balance to whatever we are facing, whichever side of the vicissitudes we are on.

Another common response to pain is wanting to get a shovel and excavate it—to get to the source of the issue. This is not a casual thing. When I enter this mode, I am determined to leave no trace of the cause of suffering; I will jump into its pit and dig out the roots. But no, that's not good enough. I put down kerosene, char the earth so that pain and old suffering will never grow again. I imagine that if I do that thing called "letting go," the old pain will be gone—totally wiped out, with no mark left on me. I believe excavation will make me whole and flawless. I will be myself, but without the defects of my trauma and pain; I will be wise, courageous, patient, and strong, never unsure, fearful, overwhelmed, or erratic. I will be able to do all the challenging things I've dreamed of.

A helpful image for these old hurts and patterns of reaction is that of moles or freckles on our skin. These are the marks that come from living our lives. Everyone has some mark on their skin, and sometimes we notice them, and sometimes we don't. Just the way we know we have a mole or a birthmark, we can know from our past experiences that we have the tendency to hide when someone is angry or the tendency to become melancholy on Sunday afternoon. We don't have to jump into the pit of self-excavation; we can understand that these tendencies are opportunities to meet ourselves with understanding.

When we look at our habits in this light, they become a part of us. Just like we see a freckle each day and know it's there, we can see these old habits as part of our life story—not a big deal. Sometimes our wounds act up, and sometimes they don't. When we don't accept ourselves and our past, chances are we won't accept others either. We'll always want them to be different. Accepting what is doesn't mean we welcome or bury it. It means we don't waste time.

When we believe we need to fix ourselves and our kids, we are doing violence. We clearly are not good enough as we are, and neither are they. When we can't accept ourselves and instead strive to make ourselves into a new and improved version of ourselves, one without our childhood experiences or wounding, we are setting ourselves up for more suffering. This well-meaning drive for self-improvement, when directed at children, can send a message that they are not acceptable as they are and need to be "fixed" or problem-free to be worthy of love.

We cannot see all the causes and conditions that create our bodies and minds. So much is mysterious, and yet we have a drive to get to the bottom of things. We don't tolerate mystery and unfairness.

This aversion to what is also manifests in our subtle or not-so-subtle molding of our children. We do not want them to be sick, anxious, or to suffer. We may want them to be always affectionate, athletic, neat, independent, good students, diligent, calm, obedient, and capable. Clinging to these desires can set up a painful situation marked by resistance and control. This is the shadow side of self-help, that relentless pursuit of invulnerability that comes in the disguise of healing. What it is—is intolerance.

Every single experience belongs to us—those we want to keep, and those we want to see drain away. The drive to "get rid of" can be understood as an aspect of Mara. In Buddhist texts, Mara is the personification of thoughts and actions that keep us caught in suffering. Mara is the sly one who sows seeds of doubt and distraction in our minds. Mara was present on the night of the Buddha's awakening, trying to distract him from his path by tempting him with beautiful women, intimidating him with fearful armies, and seeking to make the Buddha doubt he was worthy of enlightenment. Mara comes in many disguises: a false sense of kindness that leads to laziness, the enticement of living for sensual pleasure, or the encouragement of envy in the face of someone else's success. To defeat Mara, the Buddha and other practitioners use the phrase, "Mara, I see you," when they recognize the voice that leads away from the path. When we can see where our thoughts are taking us, Mara loses his ability to pull us into pain. Then we can release the hand of Mara and return to our path with confidence. We can remember that our experiences are not somehow doled out according to what we deserve and, in doing so, release stress and suffering. The extent to which we can see our life as a result of influences beyond ourselves is the extent to which we can find peace and balance.

Awareness of Impermanence

Socially engaged spirituality teacher Donald Rothberg talks about his own practice of contemplating impermanence for five minutes every day. We can notice impermanence by paying attention to the shifts in our body, mind, and emotions or noting the beginning, middle, and end of sounds around us. Rothberg did this daily for years and recommends the practice for its ability to free us from the delusion of permanence. Reflecting on impermanence in my day, I see that the morning is now sunset. Gray clouds are gathering on the horizon. My body is different than it was. I am not hungry the way I was around four o'clock today. I'm a bit sleepy, and I need to turn on a light because it's now dark. I hear the refrigerator make a noise, then stop. There's an engine; now it's gone. My spouse just came in through the garage door. I hear footsteps; now I don't.

Thich Nhat Hanh tells us, "Because of impermanence, everything is possible." I speak English and poor Spanish. With impermanence, maybe I can speak better Spanish; if I don't practice, I'll speak even worse Spanish. Impermanence makes learning possible. My dog's leg can heal in an impermanent world, babies can grow, and buds become leaves that feed everything around them. Our children change from a cluster of cells on our first sonogram into a baby, a child, and hopefully an adult. Opportunities to notice how all things keep changing are everywhere.

EXERCISE

Invitation to Practice Noticing Impermanence

This practice works best if you find a consistent time each day to check in.

1. Set a timer for five minutes.
2. Calm and settle the body with your breath or by noticing the stillness inside yourself.
3. Using your eyes, notice what's here now. Has it changed from how it was? What is the light like in your room? What time of day is it? Where are you in the room?

4. Notice sounds. Are they constant, or do they change?
5. Notice the body. Are you warm or cool? Is the body the same as it was a day ago, two hours ago, or different? Are you full, hungry, thirsty, tired, or just right?
6. Notice thoughts. Is the mind busy or peaceful? Are you worried about your child? Is it the same worry as yesterday, or has something changed?

You may like to take a few notes to remind yourself what today was like. Although there may be something difficult today, it will not be exactly the same as yesterday. When we understand impermanence, we can recognize that we, in our parenting or outside it, will not encounter the same struggle as the same person over and over. The world is changing, subtly and imperceptibly or dramatically and suddenly, and we are changing as well.

With awareness of impermanence, we know we can affect change, but we are not owned by the conditions of this embodied existence. We are free to become what we choose. When we get comfortable with impermanence, we can see the preciousness of the time we have in this body, with our kids, and on this earth, in all its pleasantness and unpleasantness. This lifetime is our classroom for waking up from the oh-so-serious ideas of ownership and identity. When we see through the veil of permanence and recognize the delusions with which Mara attempts to keep us locked in suffering, we lose identification with I, me, mine and recognize that we are all just visitors. Let us take good care of these borrowed bodies, this family, and this lovely home, our earth. Let us appreciate our children, right now.

CHAPTER FIVE

Meditation to Nourish Our Stability

Enlightenment is becoming intimate with all things.

—DōGEN

Well-being Is Possible Even in Crisis

For many parents, meditation can be the foundation of solidity. One parent of a child in distress told me, "The teachings of meditation saved my life. I needed something to help me cope. I told my husband, 'This is too hard, I can't do it.' Then I started seeing impermanence, and things started to get better." Training in meditation can give us the opportunity to cultivate and access the stillness and resilience that is always internally available, regardless of external events. As we return again and again to the present moment, we learn that we do have some choice about our thoughts. We can respond and react to whatever's happening with our kids out of conditioned habit patterns, or we can pause to observe with compassion and wisdom. Profound changes in the body and mind begin with simple awareness of the breath.

Meditation is a way to be with what is in our mind, heart, and cells without hiding our pain. It points the way to greater capacity for resilience and wellness. It is not wallowing in our feelings or being overcome by them; meditation is an active way of showing up for ourselves when we feel distress about what's going on with our child. If we have the emotional stability to support a meditation practice, our capacity for resilience and balance will likely increase. Our meditation practice will support our life and our relationship with our kids by helping us to comfort and accompany rather than suppress or run from our feelings.

As we learn to cultivate one-pointed awareness, we develop the ability to place the mind where we choose. This means it becomes possible to send ourselves understanding and comfort when we are exhausted instead of bracing against how terrible the day will be with so little sleep. The ability to choose our thoughts can give us freedom from automatic responses and conditioned habits of worry and fear.[1] When we meditate, we can even stay with the assault of circular thoughts about how to change and fix our child's situation. In either form of meditation—focused concentration or sitting in the midst of our lives and openly accepting all that is arising—we learn to stay with our intention to be present and to resist the drive to start the planning, rehearsing, thinking, and analyzing that parents do so well.

Committing to a meditation practice can give us insight into the impermanence of situations and support what is called "distress tolerance," which allows us to gradually increase our ability not to abandon ourselves when we experience the unpleasant and unwanted in our child's life. I acknowledge that when my kids are in distress, I can quickly believe my worrying will do something. I think if I keep turning their situation over in my mind, I am helping. When I stop and feel how tense both my body and mind are, I can start to release this habit of worry and recognize that ruminating is not helping them or me.

In My Life: My first experience with meditation was before I had kids, when I took an eight-week class at a local yoga center. Fed up with trying to fill the loveless hole inside me by becoming the best jewelry designer on the planet, I was willing to see what meditation could offer. The teaching was in the Kundalini Maha yogic tradition and used one mantra, "om," on the inhale and another, "ram," on the exhale. We focused on breathing these words through the third eye in the middle of the forehead.

For me, this type of meditation was heady. I escaped into a blissful state, seeing colors and images. I tried to keep practicing after Bella was born; while I found the act of meditation restful, it was like checking out. It didn't help me feel more compassionate or solid. It made me cranky when I was interrupted by the baby crying or one of motherhood's thousands of tasks. Eventually, I stopped this type of meditation and started resting in present-moment awareness instead, simply because I couldn't get away to sit and meditate the way I had been taught.

When James was born, I could notice the sensations of holding him and nursing in a different way. Understanding that this time would not last, I truly took in the feeling of his baby body, the weight of his form, his warmth, and how my body responded to his. Not quite consciously, I was tuning into mindfulness—the ability to be with what is happening in this moment. Mindfulness of the body is the first foundation of mindfulness as taught by the Buddha.

When I discovered the Plum Village tradition founded by Thich Nhat Hanh and began to tune into my body as meditation, I quickly felt more grounded. Instead of flying away into space and colors, I came back to simple breath, steps, and what my hands were doing. This gave my motherly duties more clarity and meaning. Washing dishes, I noticed the warm water, the smell of the soap, and the sounds of plates and silverware in the sink. I began to attune to the sensory world and live in the present instead of longing to be sequestered in a cave where I could concentrate enough to go on a mental vacation. Body- and breath-centered meditation helped me be more present and to feel patience and spaciousness in my life and with my kids.

After my first, very trippy meditative experiences, I found solidity in concentrating on the breath and following the steps of the Anapanasatti Sutta. The Anapanasatti Sutta is the earliest recorded meditation instruction from the Buddha, and it includes breath awareness, calming and relaxing the body, and instilling joy in the body and the mind. The description of meditation I like best is "Learning to bring our mind to rest on one point."[2] After hearing some good advice, "Pick a meditation and stay with it," I did this meditation daily for about eight years. If I flit around and practice a little bit of this and that, I won't go very deep, and the practices won't have the value that they do if I commit to them. Over the years, I have loosened up about having just one focus of meditation. I do believe staying with one type of meditation is important for starting and continuing a practice. This consistency gives a baseline and helps you to notice shifts like, "Oh, I could breathe with anxiety today without feeling worried it would last forever. I saw it melt and soften."

Eventually, I recognized I had little friendliness toward myself and spent several years sending myself *mettā*—loving kindness and absolute regard—in my late forties. I've long used a forgiveness meditation daily, and I've leaned heavily on equanimity phrases when I felt destabilized or my kids were struggling. Walking meditation, which I do whenever I need to remember I belong to the earth and the earth is still there for me, saved me from transmitting more generational trauma to my children.

Now, after twenty-some years of meditating and experimenting with different forms, I think of it as mental hygiene. If I don't meditate, I find myself mentally cloudy, more reactive, and easily irritated. Meditation also helps me to soften and hold the pain and suffering I encounter. It gives me a bigger container for my experience—a river to dilute the salt of suffering rather than a mere cup of water—and is the primary way I show up for myself. I accompany myself in meditation as a faithful and loving friend.

Meditation: Beginner's Mind and Keeping It Fresh

Buddhists talk about something called "Beginner's Mind." This is the mind that sees everything as a new and unique experience. When we practice for a while, this freshness may wear off and we may need to fall back in love with meditation. We may need to remember what it felt like to do it for the first time. I remember interning at an urban high school. I introduced a small group of freshmen to meditation and led a guided visualization using Thay's imagery of being a pebble falling through a rushing stream and then finding its home in the sandy riverbed to rest in ease while water flows fast all around. We stayed mentally on the riverbed for some time, simply observing the water moving by and resting the mind on the breath in the body. At the end of the meditation, one student opened her eyes and looked slowly around the room and then back to me. "Do people know about this?" she asked me earnestly.

In meditation, things come up. When we stop moving, acting, and relentlessly doing, the body is still, and the mind has the opportunity to rest. Sitting in meditation can be like looking beneath the bed, the place where we've shoved all the things too ugly or shameful to be seen in daylight. For some of us, meditation is a way to clear the mind and to be with what is often too deep and painful to share or even consciously know. In the space created when we slow down and touch our stillness, unwanted thoughts, emotions, fears, or memories may appear. This can lead to vulnerable and difficult moments while we confront what we would rather not, perhaps touching fear about our child or the intensity of deep mourning. Hopefully, we learn to care for these emotions and thoughts without becoming overwhelmed. When we can open to what is arising, we develop the inner strength to be with what is and create a safe place to hold all of our feelings and experiences.

I want to highlight that meditation is always an experiment. In general, there are two different ways to meditate. Most of us are familiar with focused attention (FA) meditation, in which we concentrate on one anchor such as breath, body, sound, or an image. The second way of meditating is called open awareness (OA), and in this kind of meditation we open our sense doors—hearing, feeling, seeing, smelling, tasting, and thinking—and notice the interplay of whatever arises without trying to control or shift the experience. This is called mindfulness meditation. When you practice both forms of meditation, you are applying mindfulness. Meditation can be thought of as a mindfulness delivery system.

Meditation is not a one-size-fits-all practice. When we practice, we are always in choice. When we meditate, we can ask, *How is this for me?* In doing so, we learn to trust this practice and ourselves. For some, breath is a wonderful, comforting refuge; for others, focusing on breath creates anxiety and increased agitation. If what arises in meditation is destabilizing, frightening, or overwhelming and we find we are pulled into increasing sorrow and helplessness, we can choose to find something else that supports our solidity and increases our confidence that we can show up to care for our child and ourselves. If it's overwhelming to look inward, don't push—responding compassionately to how we are is the most important consideration.

In the work I do with teens, many with diagnoses and behavior similar to my own child, using calming and soothing body scans is useful for some; for those with more trauma or body dysmorphia, even the thought of paying attention to the body causes panic. Externally focused practices, Zentangles, poetry, mindful listening, or watching clouds are ways to meditate without focusing on the body. There is no uniform practice that fits everyone. When we learn to listen to what we need, the delivery system of meditation becomes secondary to embodying compassion for ourselves in all moments.

Befriending the Mind

One of the basic ways I have learned to practice kindness and compassion during meditation is to understand the beneficial action of the thinking mind. The mind works tirelessly to take care of us and others. It is highly evolved to problem-solve, to move us and our children away from suffering, and to create positive and comfortable states for us and those we care about. When I sit down to meditate and tell the mind to stop doing what it is so brilliant at, it's like trying to pasture a racehorse in a playpen. It's not going to be a good fit. Just because I've made this arbitrary container doesn't mean my mind is going to give up its job, stop problem-solving for my child, and lie down for a nap. In fact, the more constricted and repressed the mind feels, the more it busily tries to engineer a way out—it does not want to lose its leadership position and will let me know in no uncertain terms that while I may put my body in a specific posture, I am not the boss of my mind.

The mind wanders; that is what minds do. They constantly look for strategies and ways to care for us and our kids. When we notice that the mind has wandered from our meditation, we can smile, recognizing the way that this mind is seeking to care for us and our children. This noticing—although it may feel like failing—actually strengthens the mental process of meditation. When we notice and gently bring the mind back to our object of contemplation without sending ourselves messages of blame and shame, we create new neural connections of patience and kindness while strengthening our ability to concentrate.

Our habits of mind have developed over years and decades, and these habits are often the result of early adaptive strategies we used to respond to childhood difficulties. We can look at these behaviors with our Dharma eyes and see if they lead us to happy or unhappy destinations. Do my patterns and habits of mind support me and my intentions, or do they cause me more pain? This is an ongoing question to ask in the process of learning to look with kindness and interest at our mental responses.

There's a Zen story about the willfulness of the mind. A man is galloping through a town, tearing down the streets, clinging to the neck of a speeding horse. A cowering pedestrian yells, "Where are you going in such a hurry?" The man shouts as he speeds by, "I don't know. Ask the horse!" The runaway horse is the uncontrolled mind that gallops in reaction to all the stimuli thrown its way. When we learn to meditate, we start to observe our habits of mind and notice our reactivity. We learn we don't have to do the first thing that pops into our minds. We can gently let the mind know that although we appreciate its heroic, tireless efforts to manage our children and think its way out of problems, its skills are not required right now. In short, it's out of a job. I like to tell my mind, "Thank you for trying to keep me safe. Thank you for caring so much. You must be tired. Please sit and rest with me." The mind, just like me, seems to appreciate being seen for its positive intention and cooperates much more readily when I offer understanding than if I try to willfully control or suppress my thoughts.

I also learn about befriending the mind from the experiences of those in my community. Louisa is a friend who transformed her relationship with worry. She is a regular meditator and the mother of Sebastian. She's learned that "You need to take care of yourself as much as the child." When her son's concussion didn't resolve for two years, Louisa found that the support of friends helped her reconnect with happiness. She values her friends as "better than a counselor, because they understand your pain." She talks about the shift that happened when she allowed herself to spend time with friends despite her child's difficulties. "My friend called and said, 'You are going to a show.' It was a show at a restaurant ... a comedian. At dinner I felt so isolated. Everyone was happy but me. But when the show started, I laughed so hard I cried. I had forgotten how to laugh." When we are faced with continued pain—our own and our child's—we forget how to laugh. We forget that happiness is available to us, even in the midst of this. Sometimes we need others to remind us that life holds much more than suffering. We need to remember that we are lovable and loved, even when things are beyond our control.

The Brain on Meditation

Over the last fifteen years, scientists have increasingly studied the phenomenon and impacts of meditation, and magnetic resonance imaging (fMRI) data about what happens to the brain while meditating. Neuroscientists have tracked changes in brain structure and function. We now know that when we continually activate a specific pattern of thought or emotion, the corresponding areas that register that thought or emotion in the brain get larger. This is neuroplasticity—the brain changes with training, whether this training is conscious or unconscious. Our brains are constantly responding to our lived experiences.

If you do not choose to train your brain, the world will do it for you. What you practice, you get good at. Everything we see, hear, read, feel, and process—all the messages of the world—shape our predictive minds. We can outsource this shaping to a marketing algorithm developed to exploit our insecurities or to a twenty-four-hour news cycle designed to stimulate primal fear, or we can put in the effort to make our minds a place we want to live. We have a choice: keep running the loop of fear and reactivity in our parenting, or try something else.

The use of functional MRIs is creating new awareness of how much we can affect the brain. One study in particular has profound meaning for parents: after an eight-week training for new meditators, researchers found the region of the brain correlated with empathy and compassion increased in size. Meditation training helped structure the mind to include more compassion and empathy—both essential ingredients for parents.[3]

Another discovery showed that, contrary to what we may think, knowing and feeling pain actually lessens discomfort. People who meditate feel less pain and return to baseline faster than non-meditators when given the same painful stimuli.[4] This means that when we suppress and try to minimize the pain we feel by going to war with ourselves, we actually increase our discomfort. Insisting on seeing only the silver lining, hiding our feelings about what's happening with our children, or rushing through our feelings to find a solution ultimately leads to greater pain.

Personally, I am drawn to meditation. It usually isn't hard for me to sit still unless my body is going through stressful times and I can't get comfortable. I am the child of people who value meditation, and I enjoy practicing meditation in groups. I have never regretted meditating, never thought afterward, *Well, that was a waste of time; I could have been folding laundry and really accomplished something.* Meditation reorganizes the scattered and frayed parts of my mind into a recognizable pattern and rhythm. The thoughts that looked so wild and big become just ideas that bounce around: *Oh, there's fear; I certainly know you.* I've become intimate with my own mind and thoughts.

This lived experience is supported by a study from Harvard Medical School. After an eight-week mindfulness meditation class, the amygdala—the alarm center of the brain—shrunk in meditators. These folks activated the fear center less and it got smaller; they felt safer after learning and practicing meditation for eight weeks.[5] When we learn to stay steady with the wild rides of our mind, we start to have more trust and confidence. My meditation often contains the personal vow, "Even if Bella crashes and the worst happens, I will be here for you. I will be with you. I am on your side." I need to remind myself of that. I am here for me.

Obstacles to Meditation

Where to begin? Buddhist texts refer to a number of common traps we may fall into, often called *hinderances*. These are obstacles that keep us from waking up to our true nature of interconnection and balance in this lifetime. The first is sensual desire. In this context, sensual desire covers everything from suddenly wanting a grilled chicken sandwich after being vegan for seven years to romantic and sexual fantasies, like those that might suddenly arise while you're on retreat and you become convinced you've discovered your soul mate—that person you've never spoken to, but somehow you just know by the way they sit silently on a cushion that they're the one.

The next hindrance is ill will, irritation, or anger. Sometimes my inner teenager gets pissed off at being bossed around by a retreat schedule or simply by life. Or I may suddenly get angry about how many emails I have or the muddy tracks the UPS driver left in the lawn. This anger blocks my ability to meet myself—I'm too busy for that! On the other side of the spectrum, sloth and sleepiness can also be a hinderance. You know, those times when you feel like you're a bowl of pudding. This is a big one for parents; there's always too much to do, even if the kids aren't sick or needing extra attention. When you live with babies, getting enough rest is like trying to track Bigfoot. Some days, I am lucky if my meditation practice involves breathing three times before I drive, or staying with my steps for a single stair's length. The fourth hindrance is the opposite of sleepiness and lethargy:

restlessness. This is the itchiness to move and to do, to go to that sale on Doc Martens, to surprise your friend at work with flowers. The restless mind can argue, "That would be much more beneficial than meditating, right?" But the most sticky hinderance for me is the last one: doubt. Doubt can catch me. Is meditating going to be worth the time? Should I really give up whatever else I could be doing—weeding the garden, organizing my office, or doing my taxes? I can doubt that I am ever going to feel any better. I can doubt that I am worth investing in. It was a big learning for me to recognize that part of me had resistance to sitting because it was just so much more comfortable to twirl the mind in worry; it actually felt more ordinary to feel anxiety than to attempt to take care of myself.

Changing behavior to form a new habit can elicit big resistance and discomfort, but remaining faithful to the process of overcoming the various hindrances is worth it. This is why sitting or meditating with a community or in a Sangha is so helpful. We lean on each other and inspire each other to keep going. I am fortunate to practice in community, where I am with others who value showing up to accompany themselves in meditation no matter how raw or scattered they are. When we meditate together, there is a concentrated energy that supports us all. If I am feeling shaky or distracted, I can open my eyes and see my friends sitting beautifully; this helps me to simply return to my own experience, knowing it is okay to be as I am. Sometimes, they will be the ones who need this support to keep going. I meet with a local Buddhist Sangha weekly and with a group of the Engaged Order of Interbeing members once a month.

Over the years, the folks in my spiritual community have become true friends, the ones who inspire me to keep going, keep deeply looking, keep quieting my mind and embracing my feelings. They are the ones I can talk to about the real things, and they have enough solidity to listen to my pain without being overwhelmed or trying to make it disappear. And I get to be there for them too. I talk to an empathy buddy once a week. This is a friend I trust, one who I can tell how I want to be listened to: Am I looking for simple presence or for reflection and perspective? They are able to respond with sensitivity to my vision of empathy, not theirs, and to resist judging what I need. Sometimes, after I feel heard, they help me come up with strategies or concrete actions I can take. Mostly we talk and listen, taking turns so we each feel heard and accompanied. If you can find someone in your life to listen to you and who you can listen to, this is great support and a way to deepen friendship.

A Sangha friend of mine sits every morning with a partner. They take turns calling at 6 a.m., and then they sit in silence with their phones on speaker for thirty minutes. Having that accountability and companionship, even in silence, helps draw a line around that time and make it sacred. Sometimes, though, we simply can't get this time for ourselves. It's okay when things don't follow our schedule. That's when we get to see some benefits from our practice. Do we react with rage and frustration because, yet again, our projects have been interrupted, or have we been offering ourselves enough care that we can let go of clinging to checking off the box of meditation and instead show up mindfully where we are needed? Once, sitting in meditation, I felt a soft *thud* on my head, a gentle *thunk*, and then another. I opened my eyes to see my six-year-old son standing next to me, gently raising and lowering an inflatable baseball bat rhythmically onto my head. "You wanted me?" I asked. He sighed and looked at me with exasperation, "Yeah."

These days, and especially after the isolation of the COVID-19 pandemic, I can have some laziness about meditation. My number-one excuse is that I am already too busy, and I can't stop doing whatever is so important to just sit. What works best for me is me sitting up in bed first thing in the morning and meditating before my feet touch the ground. A colleague calls this "beditation," and it's been a reliable way to keep me in alignment with my intention to meditate daily. You can even do this for the duration of a snooze cycle after your morning alarm goes off.

In My Life: At each choice point in my daughter's life, I've tried to do what was best. I sent her to a small school because she was so anxious and overwhelmed, holding onto my leg and hiding her face when we visited our local preschool. I attempted to challenge her shyness in what I believed were achievable ways: sleepovers, teams, and encouraging connections with friends. Looking back, I have no idea if taking her out of the bigger school and giving her more protection helped or simply fed her fear of socializing. I may have sent the message that she wasn't able to meet the challenges of her life. I don't know if the lack of self-worth I felt for years contributed to her drive to be accomplished and flawless. I just don't know. When I can be with this trembling worry and regret in an openhearted way, I suffer less. With the support of a meditation practice, I can experience these feelings with care and concern instead of being tormented by them. If I knew then what I know now, maybe I would have chosen differently. Maybe not. It's no reason to send myself into mother-jail.

I show the kids I work with what I mean by staying steady and accompanying by cupping my left hand and making a fist with my right hand. I then let my fist rest in the hollow of my left hand. The right hand doesn't pull the left hand out of balance; it simply rests in the palm of the upturned hand. This is the same way you support yourself and rest on yourself. If I find that place of ease and quiet, I can really become still and touch into *shamatha*, calm concentration.[6] I can develop the ability to observe and care for my mind-states without leaving this calm stillness. Staying in a place of open acceptance, I have room for the entirety of my experience as it arises; I don't have to hide.

One of the phrases I like to practice with in meditation is, "What if nothing is wrong?" It really challenges me to let go of my planning and fixing mind. And I mean it: What if, in the big picture, nothing is really wrong, even with so much I wish was different? What if I can drop the idea of wrongness? This question hits me with instant peace and lets me release some suffering.

Meditation allows me to meet places of doubt and fear in myself with deep listening and to care for the longings of my heart. Somehow, I always feel different, calmer, after meditation. Things that seemed insurmountable are now smaller, and often I find a sweetness, a place of love that opens to hold all of my experience with softness. It can bring me to tears to stay with my pain and truly accompany myself. When I see that I have something to offer myself, I remember I have something to offer others.

Community, or Sangha, is an essential part of my meditation practice. Because my child struggles with mental health issues, my spouse and I have carefully considered who we choose to share this information with in our social circles and families. Not everyone has the capacity to hold this information with sensitivity and understanding the way we would like. The stigmas and prejudice surrounding mental health diagnosis and self-harm are real. Gossip and reputation may affect our child's opportunity to get jobs and be trusted and may put her friendships at risk. Our child is free to tell the people she feels safe with about her experience. While I know I am acting from a desire to protect, it can be immensely draining for me to keep this information private and not disclose how impacted I am when my child is struggling or hospitalized. It is important to have a safe space of care where I can disclose this information and receive empathy and support so I know I am not alone.

The ability to be present for someone else's pain is cultivated in the Plum Village practice of Dharma Sharing. We listen to each other without trying to fix, change, or give advice. We agree to respect confidentiality and secondary confidentiality, which means I ask permission from the speaker if I want to talk to them later about what they shared. This double confidentiality creates safety and a place where I can unburden my heart without endangering my daughter's relationships.

I also have good friends outside the Sangha I can call. They are mostly folks who have been through difficulties with their child or children. Sometimes they listen, and sometimes they tell me about their struggles. When I hear that others have been through similar experiences, and often with more severe consequences, I remember that what can feel so personal is simply suffering—not mine, not my child's, but just suffering manifesting in this world and rippling through each life. It is part of this life, as is joy. Knowing I am connected to others in pain lets me see that I am not alone; others are walking this path with me. They have my back.

The Earth Elements

Meditation supports the ability to be with everything and to cultivate joy amidst suffering, whether we practice alone or with others. The Buddha used the elements of the natural world as meditation objects for spaciousness, calm, and solidity. These elements can help us to ground and gain perspective when we encounter suffering in our child or in ourselves. Each element offers us a doorway to balance. The Buddha uses these elements to point to our nonself nature and reminds his son, Rahula, in the Maha-Rahulovada Sutta: The Greater Exhortation to Rahula that all things, even this body and mind, are "not mine. This is not myself. This is not what I am." He urges Rahula to "develop the meditation in tune with earth" and with the other elements of water, fire, wind, and space.[7]

These elements are physically part of our bodies. When we reflect on the basic composition of minerals, the hardness of bone in the body as well as hair, nails, and teeth, we can touch the earth element and recognize that we are not separate from this planet. When we reflect on the liquidity in the body in the form of blood, sweat, fat, tears, saliva, mucus, and urine, we see we are not separate from water, clouds, fog, or vapor. The fire property is evidenced by the homeostasis that keeps the body warm and the digestive energy that converts food into fuel. The wind element is the movement of breath, the circulatory system, intestinal gases, and all animated systems. Seeing the movement of air, we understand the body is not a separate entity apart from the weather of the earth. The final element, space, is found in the hollows of the body, the internal spaces, and in all passages that get filled with breath, food, blood, fluid, and excretions.

We have much to learn from the behavior of these elements. The earth, for example, does not discriminate between what is clean or unclean; the earth accepts and transforms whatever is poured on her: "She is not horrified, humiliated, or disgusted by it."[8] She composts garbage, turning it back into fertile soil. Given enough time, the earth can clean and transform all filth, pollution, and detritus. Think of all the life and death, the pain and joy this planet has witnessed. The awareness that we are part of the earth helps us to recognize that we belong. With this knowledge, we can stay steady with illness or loss. The earth is immune to wanting only the good stuff. Resting in the strength of the earth elements in us can allow us to access impartiality and the strength to stay in the midst of difficulty with our child. We can find the mountain nature of solidity in ourselves.

Since we all respond differently to different meditations, I offer a variety of practice options for you to explore. In my own practice, I've found meditations on space and the earth especially helpful when I am feeling untethered and confused. Please experiment with these meditations. Discover which ones help you find spaciousness and solidity.

Meditation on the Elements

The Buddha instructed his son, Rahula, to meditate on the elements in the world to find balance and acceptance with all the conditions of the world, from enjoyment to horror.[9] For parents, this means balance in the times our kids are well and happy and in the times when we are unsure and doubtful about their future.

EXERCISE

Invitation to Practice Meditation on the Elements

For these meditations, you are invited to sit solidly on the earth. You may be in a chair or on a cushion. If you are in a chair, please use a wide stance to open the pelvis and increase solidity; sit on the edge of the chair with both feet firmly planted on the ground. Bring your attention to the body and the space the body occupies.

EARTH MEDITATION PRACTICE

1. Sit solidly on the earth.
2. Breathing in and out, notice the length of the body from the top of the head to the toes of the feet. Then notice the depth of the body, the volume from the front body to the back body. Inhaling, feel the width of the body, filling the lungs to touch the ribs and feeling this area of expansion from shoulder to shoulder.
3. Feel the places of earth's solidity in the body: bones made from the minerals of the earth; salt in the blood; calcium in the teeth, ribs, and spine.
4. Consider how the earth withstands heat, cold, floods, and storms and remains solid and strong.
5. Know you are connected to the earth. You are solid and stable. I am made from earth. You are earth resting on earth.
6. Put down this book, and feel the effects of this truth.

WATER MEDITATION PRACTICE

1. Sit solidly on the earth.
2. Breathing in and out, notice the length of the body from the top of the head to the toes of the feet. Then notice the depth of the body, the volume from the front body to the back body. Inhaling, feel the width of the body, filling the lungs to touch the ribs and feeling this area of expansion from shoulder to shoulder.
3. Feel the places of water's liquidity in the body: saliva in the mouth, fluid in the blink of the eyes. Consider how you've consumed water today. There is water in each cell of your body.
4. This water in you is ancient. It has been ice, a cloud, and rain. This water in you will never die, it will simply transform.
5. Know you are connected to water; You are able to adapt and move. You are made from water. You are flexible and enduring.
6. Put down this book, and feel the effects of this truth.

FIRE MEDITATION PRACTICE

1. Sit solidly on the earth.
2. Breathing in and out, notice the length of the body from the top of the head to the toes of the feet. Then notice the depth of the body, the volume from the front body to the back body. Inhaling, feel the width of the body, filling the lungs to touch the ribs and feeling this area of expansion from shoulder to shoulder.
3. Feeling the fire element inside you, notice the places of warmth in the body, the heat of your arms against your torso. The warmth of your hand on your skin. You are aware that the energy of the sun is in the food you eat. You eat sunlight turned to sugar by plants. Your life depends on the fire element of the sun. There is warmth and heat inside this body.
4. Consider how the fire element keeps all life fed and warm.
5. Know you are connected to the fire element of the sun. There is the energy of fire in your body. You are alive and creative, sustaining life.
6. Put down this book, and feel the effects of this truth.

WIND MEDITATION PRACTICE

1. Sit solidly on the earth.
2. Breathing in and out, notice the length of the body from the top of the head to the toes of the feet. Then notice the depth of the body, the volume from the front body to the back body. Inhaling, feel the width of the body, filling the lungs to touch the ribs and feeling this area of expansion from shoulder to shoulder.
3. Notice how the air moves from outside the body, becomes breath, and returns to become air. See that there is air surrounding you and inside you.
4. Know you have this air in each cell in your body. You are made of this air. You are free and unlimited.
5. Put down this book, and feel the effects of this truth.

SPACE MEDITATION PRACTICE

1. Sit solidly on the earth.

2. Breathing in and out, notice the length of the body from the top of the head to the toes of the feet. Then notice the depth of the body, the volume from the front body to the back body. Inhaling, feel the width of the body, filling the lungs to touch the ribs and feeling this area of expansion from shoulder to shoulder.

3. Notice the space outside the body: the space in the sky and in the room. Notice the space inside the body, in the nostrils, the airways, the stomach. There is space in the chambers of the heart, in the intestines and veins. See how this space is filled with all other elements: bones, breath, and fluid—all fill the space of the body.

4. Know that all space is stainless and pure. It cannot be marked by what it contains. It is fresh and vast.

5. Know you have space inside you and around you. You are made of space. You are open, pure, and fresh. The space inside you can contain everything in your life with ease.

6. Put down this book, and feel the effects of this truth.

CHAPTER SIX

Grandma Knowledge

After all those years looking after others, this old heart has
finally learned to look after itself. Each act of kindness a stitch
in this warm blanket that now covers me while I sleep.

—GRANDMA SUMANA, *The First Free Women:*
Poems of the Early Buddhist Nuns

Caring for Ourselves Is Caring for Others

We often overlook the simple but essential supports for our own health,
such as getting enough sleep, exercising, eating regular meals of nutritious
food, getting fresh air, and walking in nature—all the things we know are
good for us can so easily fall away when we are caught up in caring for
others. These are foundations of care that support our body, our immune
functions, and our mood; they directly impact our capacity to be present
for our child. I call these simple supportive habits "grandma knowledge"—wisdom that can get overlooked because of its humble origins.
We don't need to go to graduate school to tune in to how generations of
folks have cared for each other. I imagine that grandma who gives you a
hard hug and asks, "What do you want to eat?" The one who asks, "Did
you sleep okay last night?" and tells you, "Don't go making yourself sick
worrying. Put your feet up; you could use a rest. You aren't superwoman.
You'll be no use to anyone if you get sick." I imagine a grandma with the
wisdom of experience, who sees my own human vulnerability.

When we have slept well and are eating wisely, enjoying good health, maintaining balance in our work, and feeling reasonably happy, the family dog getting sick, while not welcome, won't cause us to lose our footing and fall apart. If, on the other hand, we haven't slept well, are getting sick, have been living on junk food or skipping meals, and are feeling consumed by work, the dog getting sick may be the weight that causes us to collapse. Imagine then how we would respond if it was our child instead of the dog that was ill and needed attention. Which level of capability do we want to inhabit?

Nourishment

Food is one of the essential things that we need to interact with multiple times a day. We all eat food to live. Food has the potential to be a source of stress or a source of nourishment on both physical and emotional levels. Friends who work in medical offices have told me they have to eat in front of a computer, grabbing bites between serving clients. My sister recently interviewed for a job at a walk-in clinic where no one in the office, doctors or staff, got a designated lunch break.

We find connection with others in food. We celebrate milestones with food: birthday cakes, the first meal in a new home, the celebratory promotion dinner, funeral lunches, and wedding suppers. All our greatest moments of transition and accomplishment are observed with food. The first food we had as newborns was delivered with human touch and warmth by breast or bottle feeding. Eating is a comfort and care delivery system as well as a way to nourish this body.

For many folks, disordered eating is a part of life. Anorexia, bulimia, deprivation, chronic dieting, restriction, binging, purging, and overexercising are all manifestations of a dysfunctional relationship with food fueled by factors as diverse as sexual assault, emotional enmeshment, loss, and perfectionism. Disordered eating was once thought to solely affect skinny, white, affluent girls (SWAG), which left other ethnic groups, people with larger bodies, older individuals, and males undiagnosed.[1] The prevalence of problematic relationships with food is increasing in non-Western countries.[2] Disordered eating is becoming a global problem, even in countries where food is scarce.

The gap between disordered eating and a healthy, nourishing relationship with food is widening and becoming harder to traverse. Many of us don't know what to eat or have trouble stopping when we like a specific food. It's easy to become overwhelmed by a thousand approaches to nutrition and diet. All this information can leave us confused and disconnected from our bodily sensations of hunger, fullness, and awareness of what the body needs. Longing for ease, we may be seduced by the trifecta of sugar, fat, and salt present in most prepared foods and end up eating packaged and fast foods.[3] We get a hit of dopamine when we consume this trio of foods. When we were hunters and gatherers, sweet and fatty foods were scarce and precious, providing life-sustaining calories. Not readily available in the wild, salt is necessary to regulate homeostasis and our ability to tolerate heat.[4] Our bodies encourage us to consume these foods. It is our biological inheritance.

Mindful Eating

We have the choice to distract ourselves and eat without awareness, to get it over with and move to the next thing, or to consider food an opportunity to be grateful for a gift received. Being a parent may mean you put yourself last and fall short on finding ways to nourish and care for yourself. A few mindful bites can let you know that even though you may feel alone, you are supported. Mindful eating is an essential practice in the Plum Village tradition; it nourishes our souls by reminding us of interconnection. Food doesn't come from a distant galaxy; it grows here, on this planet, and is a tangible way that this earth and this cosmos let us know we belong. The earth is glad we are here.

In mindful eating, we begin by looking at the plate of food. When we look, we consider all the causes and conditions that brought the food to us. Looking at an apple, we can see the sun, the earth, the rain, and the care of the farmer contained within it. Time is also something we consume. We can consider the months it took to grow from a flower to ripe fruit and include awareness of these factors when we eat.

We can give ourselves the luxury of time while we eat, noticing the color, shape, and aroma of our food. We can place the food in our mouths and notice the taste and texture while we thoroughly chew, staying with our sensations as the food changes. We can consider when we swallow food that it becomes part of us—the energy of the sun that turned to sugar inside a plant cell, the water, and minerals of the earth all contribute to our life. This is the lived experience of interbeing, the recognition that no one and nothing is separate on this planet. When we eat mindfully, we can experience the sacredness of being connected to all life, past, present, and future.

As Thich Nhat Hanh tells us, "This bread in my hand shows the whole cosmos supporting me." Mindful eating is a way to slow down and receive our food, not just as nutrition, but as a sign the world loves our life. She is supporting our life, the same way she nourishes the deer in the woods, the birds in the field, and the trees in the jungle. She provides for her children; she gives us what we need. When we eat mindfully and take in the food as a contribution to our lives, we can receive the love and care of the earth.

EXERCISE

Invitation to Practice Mindful Eating

---

1. Choose a meal where you can take your time and have some moments of silence. Sit down to eat without a book, TV, or other distractions.
2. Look at the food in front of you. Consider the colors; notice the aromas and visual appearance of the food.
3. Put one bite of food on your fork or spoon. Say its name to yourself: carrot, peanut butter, chickpea. Place it in your mouth,

and notice its taste: sweet, salty, spicy, sour, or acidic. Notice its texture: Crunchy, soft, or something else?

4. Chew thoroughly, and notice how the food changes. Stay with the taste and texture of the food.

5. Consider the efforts that brought this food to your body: the farmer, the soil, rain, air, sunshine, and time that went into growing this food. Include the person who transported the food, the one who cooked it, and how you came to have the means to have this food.

6. Notice that all these contributions, all these hands and hearts, are now becoming part of your cells. Feel the vastness of this gift supporting your life as you take another bite with awareness.

When we take time to respect ourselves enough to sit down and eat with reverence for ourselves and the food, we receive our food as a gift at every meal, with every bite. When we slow down and chew our food thoroughly, we honor the life in ourselves. We support ourselves. We recognize gratitude, knowing we have food while some do not. Slowing down, savoring, appreciating, and staying present with the food gives us a chance to be truly nourished.

In My Life: Most Americans run on too little sleep. In 2015, the American Academy of Sleep Medicine and Sleep Research Society released a response to CDC findings that adults, on average, need seven or more hours of restful sleep per night. Their research showed:

> Sleeping less than seven hours per night on a regular basis is associated with adverse health outcomes including weight gain and obesity, diabetes, hypertension, heart disease and stroke, depression, and increased risk of death. Sleeping less than seven hours per night is also associated with impaired immune function, increased pain, impaired performance, increased errors, and greater risk of accidents.[5]

Sleep disturbance is also linked to anxiety and can contribute to psychopathology and physical tension.[6]

Tiredness can make us grumpy and a misery to be around for our families. When we are stressed and living with a child in crisis, sleep can be hard to find. Everything feels harder when I am tired. In my life, too little sleep can deplete my patience and affect my memory. My temper is shorter, and my mind is quick to imagine the worst possible outcome when I'm sleep-deprived.

The most tired I have ever been was when Bella was a colicky baby. The night I brought my daughter home from the hospital, the doctor told me to wake her up every four hours and feed her because she was "floppy." He didn't want her losing weight or getting dehydrated. That night I set alarms, but Bella wouldn't wake up—I even ran water over her head, but she was too exhausted to open her eyes. In hindsight, I should have slept. That was the only night in the first six months of her life that Bella slept for more than four consecutive hours.

At Bella's first checkup, the pediatrician said, "Mom, you don't look good. Sit down." Then she asked me, "How much sleep are you getting?" I told her I didn't know. She said, "You need five hours to feel like a person." That was my goal: if I could sleep five hours, that would be heaven. Usually, the nights were brittle stretches of interspersed hope and hopelessness. A friend had given me a baby journal, and I had wanted to make notes about the charming things Bella was doing; recording these days filled with ten hours of crying interrupted by two fifteen-minute naps didn't fit my definition of charm.

My friend came to visit. "I want to see your beautiful baby," she said. And Bella truly was a beautiful baby, with a flawlessly round C-section head. She was tiny with perfectly proportional features, a little doll baby with a sorrowful expression in her big blue eyes. As my friend encircled the baby in her arms, Bella's face reddened and her mouth opened in a wail. Tears squeezed from her clenched eyelids. Flooded by exhaustion and hopelessness, I started to cry. My friend looked worriedly at both of us. "She won't stop crying," I squeaked. The shortbread my friend had brought had little power to cheer me up.

Having a baby wasn't supposed to be this hard. Was it? Everyone else had a better sleeping baby, I was sure. When I attended a meeting for the La Leche League, an organization focused on advocacy, education, and training related to breastfeeding, a mother asked me, "What's wrong with your daughter?" I was pacing, holding Bella on my shoulder. "She just cries," I explained, as scientifically as possible.

Most babies have a crying hour, somewhere around five o'clock. My daughter had crying hours. I'd hand her off to my husband, who would walk with her outside, where she cried into the woods for as long as he could stand it. My neighbor asked, "Have you heard the coyotes right around five? They've been so loud!" I offered a pained smile, "That's my daughter."

When I went back to work after four weeks, I was in a fog. I could hear my daughter's crying circling in my ears. The sounds of water running from the faucet and in the fan spinning—it all echoed with her tone and timbre of pain. Bella's voice had imprinted on my mind, and it yelled that I needed to do something. The problem was, I didn't know what. I tried to ease her colic. The doctor said it was "an immature digestive system." Since I was breastfeeding, I limited my own food consumption to protect Bella's digestion. I cut out dairy, tomatoes, broccoli, cabbage, beans, eggs, nuts, wheat, corn, chocolate, soy, and every allergen I could imagine. At one point I was eating chicken and rice three times a day in the hope that she would get some relief. Each time she nursed, Bella pulled her knees to her chest and cried. I'd rub her belly and place her stomach down on my lap to help ease her discomfort, but she just kept crying.

Nights were scary. When the sun went down and I took her to the bedroom, I felt a sense of dread. I didn't want the day to be over and my endless quest for sleep to begin. Bella didn't like sleeping on a flat surface, and when she slept with me, she woke up every hour, nursed, cried, nodded off, and then woke up again in about forty minutes to start the cycle over. I would lie in bed, on edge, wondering if it was safe to go to sleep. Could I manage to drift off before she woke up again?

The places she slept best were in her car seat, tucked in tight, and in her swing. She had a battery-operated blue metal swing with a padded seat printed with a primary-color solar system. When it arrived, I thought it was a horrible piece of furniture and wished it weren't in my house; when it became the only place my daughter would nap for more than twenty minutes, I saw that swing as the most beautiful piece of furniture we owned.

It took six months, as the doctor predicted, before Bella slept through the night. I remember the first time: I fed her at two in the morning and then woke up at seven o'clock in a panic. Was she breathing? Yes, she was alive. And me? I was alive too. I'd gotten that magic amount of sleep, five hours, and I did actually feel like a person again. For me, lack of sleep was the hardest part of babyhood. Although I've never heard of anyone dying from lack of sleep, sleep deprivation is used as a form of torture. When I don't get sleep, I am absolutely off-center.

Now that I no longer have a colicky infant, my capability to sleep or not rests with me. There are a number of things I may do when I can't sleep. Soothing rituals like a hot bath or shower before bed can help me to fall asleep. Lavender has been used for hundreds of years as a soothing relaxation aid. Spraying a pillow with a soothing scent can help us to feel safe and relaxed so we can go to sleep. We can use loving kindness phrases, such as "May I be safe and well," do relaxing body scans in bed if we are caught in rumination and repetitive thinking, or simply stay present and focus on the bodily sensations of lying in bed.

When I can't sleep, I like to feel everything that touches my skin. I notice the texture of the pillowcase against my cheek, the fabric of my pajamas, the feel of the sheets, and the weight of the blanket. I check if I can feel the air on my eyelids and nose. I stay with the outer contour of my body, which moves my focus from internal thinking to the sensation of touch and allows my mind to disengage from worry and rumination, to settle down and rest.

Skillful Means

Some nights, no matter what I do, how much I meditate, listen, and care for my feelings, I can't sleep. The worry feels too big, and as each hour slides by, I get more and more caught in whatever's going on (plus the added burden that I'm not sleeping and will surely pay for it with a day of struggle and exhaustion). Worse, I know that after one night of broken sleep, I may enter a cycle. If I fall into projecting and imagining the future, I feel sure I will never be able to find restful sleep. I will always be tired and cranky. These are the moments I use skillful means.

The Buddha used *upaya*, or "skillful means," when he talked with different types of people all over India. He spoke the language of those he was with, translating his message into talk about fire when he spoke with fire worshippers and talk about snakes when he spoke to snake worshippers. He agreed with ascetics that there is misery and pain in life. After getting their attention, he told them about his discovery of the Middle Way.[7] The Buddha always met his audience right where they were with an offer of compassion and liberation.

He also taught that there are no absolutes. Just like building immunity through vaccination, taking a little bit of what can make me ill, if dosed correctly, can also cure me. In the same way, distraction can be a skillful means. Sometimes I truly need to get out of my reality and give myself a break. The thing that makes this skillful is doing it with awareness. Instead of binge-watching Netflix without knowing what I am doing, it is possible to use distraction as medicine, understanding the dosage. Reading an engaging novel, doing a word puzzle, or watching a comedy can help release repetitive thinking about how to solve your child's problems. Experiment with your own skillful means and your optimum dosage of wholesome distraction.

In the Sona Sutta, an unenlightened monk named Sona who had been practicing walking meditation until his feet bled began to daydream about returning to his family, who now had money. The Buddha intuited Sona's thoughts and told him that too much intensive practice leads to restlessness and dissatisfaction, while too little makes us lazy.

He advised Sona to think about his practice like the strings of a lute. Too much tension and the strings sound off-key and are prone to break; too little tension and they are slack and don't make music.[8] Finding our own level of practice, knowing when we are stretched too taut and need to lighten up or when we are being too avoidant and could benefit from focused attention, is a way to attune and care for ourselves, mindful of our capacity. This skillfulness develops over time as we become our own resource. The same way we have a car manual with diagnostic guidance, by experimenting mindfully with skillful means we create a personal manual to troubleshoot our maladies. We know from experience what is grounding and comforting and what isn't.

Our practice gives us direct feedback about what helps us stay solid and fresh. We learn to attune to our foundation. Too little energy can be augmented by increasing our awareness and connectivity. When we find ourselves struggling to function, oversleeping, unable to get out of bed, or full of hopelessness, this can be a message that we need support, to change our focus, or to see the bigger picture. We can try going outside, doing walking meditation in nature, listening to the sounds of the world, tuning into the present moment using our senses, and opening to what is going on around us. We can notice that even though some things may seem ugly or be fading, there is still beauty and growth all around us. There is never just one thing. We can seek out colors that are stimulating, like fresh vivid greens or bright orange against a blue sky.

The opposite of lethargy is dispersed and frantic energy. When we are brittle, not sleeping, full of anxiety, and fearful, with lots of tension and energy in the body, we may need to take a break from doing and practice self-soothing, coming back to a singular focus. Soft clothing, scents, a warm bath, watching something entertaining, comforting soft foods, or drinking a cup of tea and really noticing the taste and scent of the tea may help us stabilize so we can regulate our nervous system. Giving ourselves warmth can help calm an overactive nervous system. The soothing touch of placing a hand on our heart and one on our belly can stimulate the neurotransmitter oxytocin, the prosocial "cuddle hormone." Sending ourselves a simple message of love such as, "I am glad you were born just the way you are," "I am here for you," or "May you know peace, even in this," is a way to come back home to balance. Your practice is for you. It is not to please anyone else. It needs to be supportive for you. Find out what works for you, and know that it may change. You can rely on your own lived experience to help you skillfully create your own scaffolding of support.

Skillful means involves finding what brings back energy, appreciation of life, and balance. You may like to broaden your awareness and offer solidity and energy to all the folks around the globe who are feeling awash in helplessness, just like us. Remembering the impersonal nature of suffering and our place in this human family, who all feel pain at some time, can reconnect us to a wider view and remind us of the naturalness of suffering. Softening to this awareness can help us open our hearts to compassion, which eases suffering.

Sometimes what's going on with our kids is really disturbing and we simply long for comfort, for a return to what was normal, or a respite from worry. What used to be a routine, predictable life seems completely out of reach. We can actively ask ourselves, "What am I longing for?" Is it fun, laughter, ease, intimacy, to be heard? When we ask this question to our body and mind, we answer. We know intuitively what we are longing for. Even knowing what we are seeking can allow the nervous system to relax. Our feelings are longing to be known and understood.

Thankfulness: Thaddeus's Story

Thaddeus is one of the most balanced and resilient people I've encountered. He considers his life blessed and often says, "I am so lucky," despite the huge suffering he has lived through. The relationship between Thaddeus and his son Richard is an example of the human ability to develop gratitude and perspective. Thaddeus recalls his father's favorite adage, "Whatever doesn't kill you makes you stronger," and his mother's optimistic explanation that "Everything happens for the best," statements he heard often during his child-hood. He credits his parents' influence, their focus on determination, commitment, and positivity, as the ground for his own resilience and emotional stamina.

Thaddeus and his wife, Lori, are both medical professionals. Even so, they were unprepared for the birth of their child. "We knew something was up when he first came out. Richard had severe club feet, and his whole lower body hadn't formed completely. When you find one anomaly, they say, look for more." The baby was taken immediately to the NICU for tests and developed meningitis the next day. Thaddeus remembers, "The doctors start pumping him full of these two antibiotics that are meant to cross the blood-brain bar-rier. They tell us one drug is probably going to make him deaf and the other will probably make him blind—but we'll save his life. We called in a priest and had him baptized and confirmed. He pulled through, but when you pull through neonatal meningitis, there is profound brain damage."

Thaddeus's family was optimistic. They encouraged him to hope for the best and believe that healing was possible. Thaddeus could see the enormity of the situation and still believed that his son would be alright. "I held on to this probably irrational hope that he was still going to develop for a long time," he remembers. As a medical professional, Thaddeus had a clear understanding of his son's development: "We were not only dealing with the brain … we were dealing with all these physical anomalies. His kidneys were not formed right. His ureters were not formed right. He had heart defects. He had a big cyst in the back of his brain. He had all kinds of things wrong."

At three years old, Richard still couldn't lift his head, and Thad-deus began to lose hope that his child would recover into the athletic son he had dreamed of playing hockey with. He came to realize that Richard wouldn't catch up in his development, and with this realiza-tion, he became enraged. "Now I'm angry. Now I'm angry at God. I mean, what's the purpose of this? Why create a being that is going to suffer and create suffering in everyone around him who watches his suffering? It just made no sense to me."

Thaddeus did not let Richard's condition keep him separated from the world. When Richard was big enough, he put him in a backpack and took him fly-fishing. He took him to the grocery store, went biking with him in a carrier, brought him to church, and, despite all the obstacles, Richard attended public school and had friends. Although he couldn't walk or speak, he could communicate with happy and sad sounds and facial expressions.

Thaddeus's suffering increased when he and his wife had a second child born with the same physical anomalies despite a chromosomal analysis from a prominent geneticist who assured them there was no risk of abnormal fetal development. The second baby, Jeff, lived for half a day. "He had hydronephrosis. His kidneys were so large his entire abdominal cavity was pushed up into his chest, so his lungs never formed. He was on a respirator and the neonatologist said, 'I don't think he'll ever come off a respirator.' 'So, basically you're telling us that his anomalies are not compatible with life.' 'Yes,' he said, 'I am telling you that.' That's when we decided to take him off the machine and hold him. He didn't live very long. I hate to admit it, but I felt some peace in letting him go. It's kind of selfish, but I couldn't deal with another child with profound disabilities."

Thaddeus felt frustration and anger at Jeff's birth and death and the relentless demands of caring for Richard. Thaddeus and Lori, a registered nurse, took shifts caring for Richard when they weren't at work. They were his primary caregivers, and the physical work of caregiving was a full-time job despite the fact that both parents had careers and needed to bring in an income. Richard could not walk, feed himself, or chew, so all his food had to be ground up. Lori made all his food herself. Richard was urinary incontinent and had a colostomy bag, since his rectum hadn't completely formed. He needed to be bathed, dressed, and undressed as well as carried and lifted from his bed to his changing table and into his wheelchair. These tasks became increasingly difficult as he got older and heavier. Thaddeus remembers, "We didn't have any life, and that pissed me off. Every time a friend said, 'Let's go get a beer,' 'Let's go to a hockey game,' I could never do it." Thaddeus entered a phase of intense pain, mourning, and anger as he saw his life being swallowed by Richard's disabilities.

Thaddeus struggled with the idea that his life, filled with the never-ending work of caring for his son, had lost focus. Over time, though, something began to shift; he saw his son in a bigger context, and his perception of Richard's disability changed. Richard touched people in a deep way and reminded them of their shared humanity. When folks encountered Richard, they became humbler and more vulnerable themselves as they connected with him.

"Here's a kid that's profoundly disabled, frustrated in many ways, and unable to communicate like a normal human being. All kinds of physical anomalies, pain, and numerous surgeries. He became our teacher. He taught us things that really matter. I always say to my patients, 'At the end of your life you're not going to want on your headstone that you had a clean house. You had a nice car. You want to know that you touched lives, that you made a difference, that you were compassionate, kind, and loving.'" Thaddeus began to think of Richard as a highly evolved soul living his life for a specific purpose, which made Thaddeus's role as his caregiver deeply important.

"Richard brought that out in people. In everyone he came in contact with. That's what happened. People just exuded compassion, care, and kindness. So that's how I made sense of it. That was Richard's gift to me and the world."

When Thaddeus saw the interconnectedness, or, as Thich Nhat Hanh calls it, the interbeing, he was part of, Richard's life took on deep value. And so did his own. The insight into how Richard's presence touched the lives of others transformed Thaddeus's perception of his and Lori's suffering. Seen through a larger lens, their collective struggle took on new meaning and became a gift to the world.

Richard lived to be twenty-three, and his parents supplied most of his daily care. Through it all, Thaddeus and Lori exhibited a resilience that kept them afloat, even when faced with tremendous loss, grief, and challenge. They did not fall into despair and become helpless. The biggest parenting lesson Thaddeus learned was to release his perfectionism and to accept people as they are without any expectation they will change. "We have to change. The situation in our lives isn't going to change, and I use Richard as an example. He wasn't changing; my life was."

There are two aspects of acceptance intertwined in these lives: the acceptance that perseveres through hardships and the acceptance that sees clearly what is happening without fighting. Thaddeus went through months and years of grief and anger before finding the wisdom to stop trying to engineer an impossible change. Through directly experiencing the compounded suffering of wishing things were otherwise, Thaddeus learned to straighten beneath the weight of his responsibilities and disappointments and to take a long view. His ability to see the life that he shared with Richard in a bigger context gave him a sense of purpose and offered recognition that this suffering had value.

We can intellectually understand that mindfulness and equanimity are based on what is and that the recognition of impermanence does not require reframing. We can know that life is the ultimate teacher. But this long view of equanimity is grown from patience and experience; it is not something we can learn intellectually or from reading a book. Instead, like coming through a storm, we embody the joy of confidence when we ride out our worst fears and find that we are still here, whole and capable. When conditions exceed our capacity to stay with what is arising, it is skillful and kind to use reframing and access the resources we have. We can draw strength from our spiritual teachers, our community, and from the knowledge that we are part of this earth. We deserve to be here.

When we are able to see the worth in our actions, to see that life, often fraught with difficulties and pain, is valuable, we can look at our actions and intentions with understanding. Our intention matters. Our caring matters. The suffering of others, even if we do not understand it and wish it were otherwise, matters. Again and again, we see that all beings share in the common heritage of pain and grace.

Our job is to show up, to care, and, just as Thaddeus learned, to allow our children to enter into our hearts. When Thaddeus saw what Richard brought to his life and to the world, he had nothing but gratitude for his presence. Richard taught the lesson of loving and allowing to everyone he met.

Nurturing Gratitude

Recognizing gratitude and cultivating it is a protective factor against depression and helplessness; it wakes up compassion and care and supports strong nurturing relationships.[9] Gratitude also feels good. The experience of gratitude awakens joy, ease, awe, and feelings of connection and support. As with any practice, when we foster a feeling of gratitude, this feeling can shift from a temporary state to a trait, a way of looking at our life.[10] Recognizing and naming what is going well with gratefulness can lift us and connect us to others. Gratitude is grandma knowledge.

The Buddha taught about the importance of gratitude as an integral part of our spiritual development. I had resistance to keeping a gratitude journal. It smacked of popular culture and self-help fixes, but then I tried it. The consistent noting of what I feel grateful for with the added question of what I did to make this possible changed my practice. It allows me to see that what I do contributes to creating conditions that nurture my life. The following is the gratitude practice I use, adapted from Jim and Jori Manske, trainers at the Center for Nonviolent Communication.

EXERCISE

Invitation to Practice Gratitude Journaling

---

1. Write down something specific someone did or an event that made your life more wonderful. For example: my friend told me

I helped her during a really hard time. I stopped walking when I saw a double rainbow and watched it. Deborah made me dinner.

2. Write down how you feel as you write the gratitude. Name the emotions you are experiencing and the bodily sensations as you consider how this action contributed to your life.

3. Write down what universal value the action contributed to: peace, safety, ease, fun, recognition, respect, trust, freedom, honesty, consideration, choice, justice, security, creativity, friendship, play, understanding, belonging, to matter, self-expression, authenticity, support, love, rest, honoring agreements, order, stability, reassurance, guidance, and so on.

4. Name what you did to help make this action possible. For example: I listened to them. I paid attention. I showed up. I bought the ingredients for dinner. I let someone help me. I've maintained a friendship with them for fifteen years. I stopped and watched the clouds. I noticed how good the food was, and so on.

5. Notice how interconnected you are with what you're grateful for. How do you feel now?

In Zen practice, this interconnection is known as "The giver and receiver are one." Pause and savor this mutuality.

CHAPTER SEVEN

Empathy and Compassion

That one who is himself sinking in the mud should pull out
another who is sinking in the mud is impossible; that one who
is not himself sinking in the mud should pull out another who
is sinking ... is possible.

—*Sallekha Sutta*, TRANSLATED BY BHIKKHU ÑĀṆAMOLI
AND BHIKKHU BODHI

Understanding Our Connection

Empathy is the cognitive ability to sense what someone else is feeling.
It's the ability to understand what it's like for someone else. A parent's
ability to empathize lets their child know they matter and that what
they feel matters. This ability is vital for creating a secure and strong
relationship. Empathy can protect children from low self-regard, loneliness, and depression. Clinical professor of psychiatry at UCLA and
educator Daniel Siegel writes that children need to "feel felt."[1] Empathy allows us to live collectively and cooperatively.

I can let my child know I get that she feels hurt she doesn't get to
play her brother's Xbox when his friends come over. I can offer understanding without explaining that her brother can choose who he wants
to play with and that we respect each other's wishes. I don't educate
when I am in empathy: I simply meet my kid right where they are.
There's a saying, "Connection before correction." If I try to explain

someone else's perspective to a child in pain, not only will the child not want to support the other person, but they will also miss my empathy. Now they have two problems: feeling bad and having a parent who doesn't understand or allow them to feel what they feel.

Though it's important to feel empathy, it is also important to stay balanced. Empathy is vulnerable. It entails accessing pain. We know what disappointment, frustration, or hurt feels like from our own lived experience. When we offer empathy to someone in pain, it can bring up our own. As parents we get hit with discomfort the first time the baby cries and we can't figure out what to do. We have all experienced our own physical and psychological pain, but for many parents, the greatest pain is witnessing our children in distress and being unable to relieve it. Staying balanced is the beginning of offering compassion, care, or support to others. If we aren't able to find this balance and show up for our children's feelings with spaciousness and solidity, we can fall into empathetic distress, which activates the neural shared pain circuitry.

As parents, understanding our child's emotions can be exquisitely challenging. We may think our child's feelings are unreasonable or that they are overreacting. It's important to remember empathy is not agreement. Empathy makes understanding possible. Please take a moment and put down this book and see how those words live in your cells. What does that mean for you to understand what it's like for them when it's so different than what you would want? What does it mean to empathize without agreeing?

A 2004 study of the shared pain circuitry in our brain shows just how sensitive we are to pain and threat in those we love. Neuroscientists recruited people in close relationships and gave electric shocks to one member of the couple while monitoring both partners' brains for activation in pain regions. (I often wonder who signs up for these studies, but I guess I should be grateful that someone is willing to get shocked for science.) When researchers told participants their partner would get an electric shock in a few seconds, participants' own brains initiated the same pain circuit as evidenced in the person actively receiving the shock, minus the site-specific locator activation.[2]

Just hearing that someone they cared about would be in pain was enough to stimulate a pain response. This involuntary shared pain circuitry creates emotional blending—feeling what someone else feels without any separation. If I am emotionally blended with my child and they are anxious, I am anxious about their anxiety. This can lead to becoming mired in shared suffering and being pulled under to a place of helplessness, depression, and burnout.[3] This is why self-awareness and balance are necessary when we attune to the feelings of others, especially if these others are our children.

Maria, a friend for over twenty years and a mother whose son survived meningitis, told me, "The darkest moment in my life was seeing my son in his darkest moment. I couldn't do anything. When he was a baby, I could hold him." Her voice shakes. "The darkest moment for a mother is seeing their kids suffer. I don't think there's a pain in the world worse than that. Your hands are tied. It's so terrible."

But there is something essential we as parents do have control over: how we see ourselves as capable or incapable of meeting the challenges of parenting in difficulty. The link between helplessness and depression is profoundly complex and includes conditioning, genetic makeup, our own histories, and lineage. The ability to act and to believe what we do matters is called agency. Simply put, agency is recognizing our choice about what we do and how our actions are felt in the world. When we are caught in the belief that our actions are ineffective and pointless, convinced that nothing we do will make a difference for our child's outcome, we are susceptible to despair and defeat, which contribute to depression.[4] It is my hope that the practices in this chapter and this book help you to find and nurture the balance and solidity that support a recognition of your own agency.

Carol's Story

Carol is the mother of one of Bella's classmates. Her story demonstrates the difficulty that arises when our natural protective desire to care for our child at all costs clashes with the reality of parental limitations. Carol's daughter, Alicia, was born with the umbilical cord wrapped twice around her neck and was in the NICU for ten days. For Carol, the birth was traumatic: "I literally almost died having her.... I was bleeding internally for twelve hours in the hospital before they figured out I had almost no platelets left." Carol was in the ICU for ten days.

From the beginning, Alicia needed extra help. "She had asthma the first two years, and we were up all night giving her albuterol. It was hard. I was very sick." Carol's body was still recovering from her surgery and blood loss, and she was doing her best to live up to the societal expectations of having a baby and an outside job. She wasn't able to take the time she needed to adequately heal her body. "We had to wake Alicia up every four hours, and I was working full-time. After a year I said, 'I can't do this anymore.'"

Carol describes her daughter as strong-willed and "not particularly affectionate. That was hard for me because I had this vision of a daughter who was all warm and fuzzy with me, and she just wasn't having that. Alicia was very independent. We went our way, though she was always a little hard, and then we hit ninth grade." Carol takes a deep breath. "I always say if I had to relive that year again, I don't think I could survive it."

Alicia was bullied by a boy in her grade who sent profanity-laced sexually threatening texts and physically intimidated her. The school tried to intervene, but other kids were caught up in the inquiry. Alicia's friends abandoned her and sided with the boy who was harassing her. Carol felt the effects of her daughter's distress. "She was an emotional basket case for the whole second half of the year, and I was afraid she would hurt herself. The worst part was one night she spent screaming in my living room, pulling her hair out. I came very close to calling 911. It was hugely traumatic for us."

Carol was living with the daily fallout of having a depressed and emotionally volatile child, constantly scared that Alicia would hurt herself. She was exhausted from endless vigilance. "I felt totally inadequate when this first started. I was in a state of panic. I think my husband was in a state of panic. I would go to work, shut the door on my lunch break, and just cry. It was awful—the stress. I did not cope with it well at all. I wondered what would next year look like, and the year after that, and the year after that."

During episodes of distress and helplessness, the belief that we are not capable of meeting the needs of our child or solving the situation creates pain. When confronted with situations beyond our control, both animals who could not escape from an electric shock and humans who received a terminal diagnosis for their child had the same response to these overwhelming, uncontrollable situations: helplessness, passivity, depression, and inaction.[5]

Carol acknowledges that she felt totally unbalanced and had no confidence in her ability to meet Alicia's needs. When we find ourselves emotionally blended with our children, all of our happiness hangs on the hope that they will be well and happy. We give away our power and pin our health and well-being to something we have no control over. We cannot cure disease in another and cannot take away our children's addictions, anxiety, or harmful beliefs. Although we can do everything in our power to create conditions that support our children, ultimately we are all the recipients of eons of genetics, conditions, and events we only partially glimpse.

For Carol, lack of connection with her own mother fueled doubts about her parenting capabilities. Carol grew up feeling that her mother wasn't there for her—she didn't even know how to comfort her when she fell. Attachment theory describes how inherited patterns of parenting affect us and how we can, for example, unknowingly transmit the same lack of connection or wholeness to our children. Carol acknowledges the confusion and helplessness she felt as a parent.

"I have a lot of self-doubt. It goes back to the fact that my own mother was a terrible mom. I never had a good role model. I feel like women who had that good nurturing mom have a big leg up on the rest of us when they have kids. They know what to do. They've seen it their whole lives. Simple things sometimes. What do you do when you skin your knee? When you haven't had that role model, it's just harder. And the funny thing is, I hardly had a mom, and my husband didn't have a dad—his passed away when he was five. So, between the two of us, we had no idea what we were doing."

Alicia is now twenty-two and has been diagnosed with ADD and anxiety. She has a processing disorder, which makes integrating new information difficult. As I write this, she had recently started a new job. After a few weeks, Alicia was called into a meeting to explain why she worked so slowly. The stigma of shame and difference surrounding psychological disorders and invisible disabilities such as ADD is very strong; Alicia didn't disclose her diagnosis. She called Carol in a panic that she would be fired. Alicia has called her mother in tears four or five times in the last six weeks. "She's always in trauma," says Carol. "She very rarely calls me when she's happy. When I see her number on my phone, I have an immediate sense of dread. *What happened now?* It's awful, and I've even said to her, 'Can you call me when you have a good day sometimes?'"

Parents who are emotionally enmeshed with their child have heightened anxiety when encountering their child. Research revealed that frequent, intensified empathetic responses without self-awareness and balance can bring about neurological changes equivalent to PTSD symptoms, increasing activation in the amygdala, the fear response region of the brain.[6] This cycle of vigilance, fearfulness, and overwhelm based in emotional entanglement makes it extra challenging to maintain balance and perspective. We remain in this cycle at the expense of our own health and well-being.

Carol recognizes that she is emotionally blended with Alicia. For Carol, constant emotional reactivity creates distrust, fear, and the impulse to protect herself. She longs for rest, trust, and ease in her relationship with her daughter.

"I was not separate from her. I am on her path with her. And I struggle with it. When she calls me and she's like this, I can't sleep. I think of her every minute of the day. I constantly text her. And it's really not that different from ninth grade. I know she has more coping skills than she used to. She went away to school. She graduated on time from a good school, which I intellectually remind myself of. But emotionally, I don't trust her to know what to do. I try not to show her I don't trust her."

Carol is overwhelmed with the enormity of her daughter's problems and wishes she had an easier relationship with both her mother and her daughter. There is constant tension between being enmeshed in her daughter's emotional life, exhausted and overwhelmed, and feeling guilty when she longs for space and ease. It requires dedication, but stability can be learned.

Forgiveness

Being human means I will make mistakes. One of the most healing and nurturing things I can do for myself is to offer the compassion of self-forgiveness. As the Sufi poet Rumi writes, "Your task is not to seek love, but to seek and find all the barriers within yourself that you have built against it." I think of forgiveness as a drop of water that, over time, can melt the ice around the heart that resists loving itself.

I am not perfect; wanting to be perfect and mistake-free causes harm. I will make mistakes raising my children. An obstacle many parents have is the idea that *I should have known better*. This makes loving or forgiving myself challenging. I work to forgive myself for what I did not know instead of blaming myself for not knowing the future. I try to remember that I did what I thought was right without knowing how things would turn out for my children. I have more resilience this way: when things don't go according to plan, I can forgive myself. I don't have to get stuck in hellish shame and blame. I can try again, without the fear of having to punish myself when things go awry with my kids.

A habit that blocks compassion is the culture of blame. In many families and societies, there is a rush to assign blame based on the mistaken belief that if we find out who is responsible, everything will be fixed. When we find ourselves getting swept up in the wrongness of an unfair situation or find ourselves obsessing over the why, this drive may stem from synthesizing blame. In the West, our justice system comprises blame and punishment. We confuse these things with actual justice and believe that shaming and punishing one person can make the pain of another person less. It's like a magical transitive property: if you feel badly about how you hurt me, I will be all better.

But it doesn't work this way. In my experience, when we blame someone, we actually end up feeling worse. Even if we could find the source of the problem, identify the aunt who carried the seeds of addiction or the great-grandfather with sickle cell anemia, who would benefit? While we do need to address injustice and hold ourselves and others accountable, assigning blame to a painful but nonetheless natural situation derails our better intentions and leads us into frustration and bitterness.

If this sounds far-fetched, take a moment and bring up a painful experience. Focus on who caused it. Notice any tension in the body. How is the belly, the breath, the jaw, the shoulders? Is the situation becoming more bearable or less? Does blame lighten the unpleasant emotion? Now recall the same incident without going into the cause. Simply notice the unpleasant feeling. Where does it manifest in the body? Ask yourself to stay with your experience as a presence of care. You may like to use the following phrases: *This is how it feels to be—disappointed, terrified, frustrated, sad, hurt, alone. I understand. I care about this feeling.* At first, showing up as a presence of care if we are not used to it may seem awkward and clunky. We may not trust that our own presence is enough. If doubt arises, we can meet this too with understanding: *Of course I feel like this. It makes perfect sense. This is brand new.* As we keep meeting what is arising with gentle determination, understanding, and kindness, we have the opportunity to change our habits and strengthen our ability to stay solid and unafraid of our feelings.

In My Life: I grew up in a house where the first words when something broke or went missing were, "Who did this?" We played the game of assigning blame and discharged anger and disapproval onto whoever made a mistake. I call it the dirty hot potato—if I pass the blame to someone else, I don't get burned. I learned that it was scary to be wrong or to mess up and that it was not okay when someone found out. I wanted to hide all my imperfections to stay safe and lovable. My mind had an extra-large dumpster to hold my shame, blame, and all the things too ugly or painful to share. This repository of shame and blame eventually kept me from accepting my own children's mistakes. I unconsciously applied this perfectionism to their lives, and all of us felt the need to hide from each other to avoid shame.

When I first encountered forgiveness practice, hearing it brought tears to my eyes. I knew forgiveness was something I longed for, but it wasn't something I had learned growing up. I had no idea how to get there. Remembering to forgive myself requires practice and repetition. It doesn't come naturally to me and requires daily reminding. I developed a meditation from the classic Buddhist forgiveness meditation. When I teach it to the kids I work with, I tell them that meditation is one drop of water that, over time, can wear through all the protection and resistance built up against seeing ourselves as worthy of our own love and support. I tell the kids that I practiced this meditation each morning for more than a year before I could start to believe it or feel forgiveness was possible. That was how thick the layer of rock was around my heart.

Forgiving myself means I stop wanting to punish myself with guilt and shame for mistakes I have made. Forgiveness means I can make mistakes and still be worthy of my love and support. It does not mean the things I did were wonderful; forgiving myself for hurting another may involve making amends and working to reestablish trust. Forgiving myself teaches me, though, that I have goodness inside me always. A friend told me, "If you knew then what you know now, you'd have done something different." Even if my intention was to help, the course I chose may have led to more pain because I couldn't see all the threads that made up the cloth.

Forgiving someone else is something I do for myself. It is not to please anyone else. Forgiveness does not have a timetable or an expiration date. Forgiveness happens after I am able to care for the hurt another person has caused. It happens when I recognize that this pain I carry in the form of judgment, hatred, and revenge has hurt me enough. I forgive when I am ready to release pain. Sometimes forgiveness means I understand the motives of another person, but it's important to separate forgiveness from approval. Forgiveness does not mean what someone did was okay, nor does it mean I must remain in contact with the person who hurt me. Forgiveness means I keep my heart open and I keep myself safe.

EXERCISE

Invitation to Practice Forgiveness Meditation

Find a quiet place where you will be undisturbed. Get comfortable, and give yourself permission to simply see how this feels for you. Take frequent pauses to notice how these phrases land in your mind, heart, and body. Find an anchor of breath or stillness. Bring some calm into the body and mind. Let yourself be open to whatever arises as you read the following words:

1. Breathing in, I bring awareness to my body. Breathing out, I forgive this body for everything I do not like or want about this body.
2. Breathing in, I recognize the ways I have hurt my body in the past, both knowingly and unknowingly. Breathing out, I ask my body for forgiveness.
3. Breathing in, I bring awareness to the ways I have hurt myself, both knowingly and unknowingly, through my thoughts, words, and deeds. Breathing out, I offer forgiveness for harming myself.
4. Breathing in, I bring awareness to the way I have hurt my child or another, both knowingly and unknowingly, through my thoughts, speech, or actions. Breathing out, I offer myself forgiveness for any pain I have purposely or accidentally stimulated in others in the past and present.

6. Breathing in, I bring awareness to the ways I have been hurt, intentionally and unintentionally, by my child or another's thoughts, speech, or actions. Breathing out, I offer them the same forgiveness I offer myself.

Expansion

1. Breathing in, I bring awareness to my body. Breathing out, I forgive this body for everything I do not like or want about this body.

Acknowledging the ways this body has disappointed me, I offer forgiveness for all the things I do not like or want about this body. I forgive my face. I forgive my skin for not being the color or texture I want, for breaking out, for wrinkles, for aging. I forgive my features: my eyes, my lips, my nose—I forgive their shape, their being too big or too small, too wide or too narrow, not the right color or look. I forgive my hair for being too thin, too thick, too curly, too straight, not the right color or texture. In this moment, to whatever degree I am willing and able, I forgive everything about my face.

I forgive my body for all the things I cannot control, for my inherited genetics, for not looking the way I want, for being too big or too small, too tall or short, for being too curvy or too straight, for being born in this body, or for not looking like the gender I am. I forgive my skin for being the wrong color or texture; I forgive my hips for being too wide or too narrow; my legs for being too long, too short, too thick, too thin, too muscular, not muscular enough. I forgive myself for getting old, for getting sick, for tiredness and pain. I forgive my body for being imperfect. I understand my body is doing its absolute best and tries to support and care for me always. To the extent I am willing, I offer my forgiveness to this body for being part of nature, just like the trees in the woods and the deer in the forest. I know this body loves me, and to the extent I am able, I trust my body.

2. Breathing in, I recognize the ways I have hurt my body in the past, both knowingly and unknowingly. Breathing out, I ask my body for forgiveness.

Dear body, I have not always listened to you. Sometimes I ignore hunger, tiredness, fatigue, and pain. I do not always care for you with exercise or healthy food. Maybe I ingested food, drink, or substances that brought toxins into my body. I hurt myself because I did not know a better way to be with my pain. Now I ask you, my body, for forgiveness for the ways I have been violent with you and have turned away from you. To the best of my abilities, I commit to caring for you and to not abandoning you. To whatever degree possible, I ask forgiveness of you, my body. Please trust me to take care of you. Just as my body loves me and always does the best it can, I promise to be there to support and care for my body.

3. Breathing in, I bring awareness to the ways I have hurt myself, both knowingly and unknowingly, through my thoughts, words, and deeds. Breathing out, I offer forgiveness for harming myself.

Sometimes, I place unrealistic expectations on myself or create impossible to-do lists that I cannot accomplish. I have been harsh and critical of my abilities. I compare myself to others and see myself as less than. Sometimes I hide my feelings and cause pain. I forgive myself for feeling scared, jealous, and anxious. I forgive myself for my anger, for my resentment, and for my judgments. I forgive myself for believing I am not worthy of love. I forgive myself for my depression.

To the extent I am able, I offer myself forgiveness for my lack of understanding of my suffering and dissatisfaction with myself. I give myself permission to be human and to make mistakes. I release myself from the prison of perfection. To the degree I am able, I forgive myself for what I perceive as imperfections and promise to love and accept myself exactly as I am right now without any expectation that I will ever be any different. To the extent I am willing and able, I vow to listen to my pain and to love and accept myself even when I make mistakes, even when I am wrong. I release myself from responsibility for other people's thoughts, feelings, and actions. I forgive myself for hurting myself. I forgive myself for not forgiving myself.

4. Breathing in, I bring awareness to the way I have hurt my child or another, both knowingly and unknowingly, through my thoughts, speech, or actions. Breathing out, I offer myself forgiveness for any pain I have purposely or accidentally stimulated in others in the past and present.

Sometimes I make mistakes and hurt others. Sometimes I want to hurt those who hurt me. Understanding that the inability to care for my suffering only brings more suffering, I commit to offering compassionate care to my thoughts and feelings so I will be capable of kindness and compassion for myself and others. I forgive myself for my past, for my actions and any harm they have caused. I know what I did was not always wonderful; to reestablish trust, I may need to make amends. I know I am capable of change. To the extent I am able, I forgive myself for my unskillfulness. I forgive myself for not knowing what I did not know.

Giving myself understanding and offering myself gentleness, I release myself as best I can from judgment, blame, and disappointment because of my unskillful thoughts, speech, and actions. I am free from the prison of perfection. I return to a place of unconditional love in my own heart.

Compassion Is a Verb

Compassion has impact. Compassion, *karuna* in Pali, is the wish to relieve suffering. This wish arises when our open heart meets pain, in ourselves or another. In Buddhist commentaries, compassion is described as a mother who will do anything for her child.[7] She will go against the wishes of the child and give bitter medicine if it heals.

There is nothing she won't do or sacrifice to help her child. Her loving intention to ease the pain of her child is visible in action. Compassion can be fierce.

Understanding how empathetic blending and compassion differ is important to keep balance in parenting. Compassion is a potent medicine for both the one who offers and the one who receives. In the Buddhist sense, compassion is action: "Compassion is a verb," Thich Nhat Hanh said. It is a relationship we engage in and a way of being. Compassion is born of cognitive empathy. It understands what pain feels like and then moves into the desire to release the other from pain.

The Buddhist tradition teaches that the basis for compassion is loving kindness (mettā in Pali). When loving kindness turns its attention to suffering, compassion is the response—an open-hearted wish to relieve suffering. Just as a parent picks up a child who has fallen and comforts them, compassion is a natural response to pain in ourselves and others. It's the way love takes form in our relationships with our children.

Studies from compassion researchers Tania Singer and Olga Klimecki used fMRI brain imaging to track one group of subjects trained in empathy while they watched video recordings of people in distress.[8] The empathy training encouraged participants to feel and join with the sadness and suffering of another. Afterward, a compassion training introduced mettā meditation. Mettā meditation is a Buddhist-based practice in which the meditator actively inclines their mind toward releasing suffering. This practice encourages an openhearted wish for well-being for all. Classically, mettā meditation utilizes phrases such as, "May you be happy," "May you be safe from all internal and external harm," "May you have health," and "May you care for yourself with ease."

The fMRI results for those trained in empathy only displayed an activation of the pain circuitry showing emotional pain, sadness, and discomfort while watching videos of people in distress. Results collected after the compassion training, however, showed activation in the areas of the brain associated with reward and pleasure. Researchers found that compassion creates warm feelings of belonging, close connection, and love, though it does not remove sadness and negative affect. While subjects still felt the pain of those who were suffering, they also felt the happiness of actively assisting with the intention to remove suffering.[9] The return to agency and the experience of making a difference came in the form of a thought—an intention. A thought is already an action. Researchers found that compassion training reversed negative feelings and brought the subjects back to baseline levels. Even short-term compassion training had the ability to remove empathetic blending and distress caused by the pain of another.

Valuing thoughts goes against our cultural ethos. We are a results-based society. We respect solutions and fixes more than intentions. But before a solution happens, it needs to be a thought. The thought is the seed of action. In Buddhism, this thought is already doing something. It can move energy in the direction of compassion, and it has value.

If we only focus on the pain our child is in, we feel it as pain. We are sad, despondent, and helpless. If we focus on our intention to relieve that pain based on our shared understanding of what pain feels like, we feel happier, more competent, and stronger. This is a very important distinction for parents, especially knowing that helplessness and overwhelm can lead to depression and despondency.[10] Even the thought that I want my kids to be well is doing something.

The Buddhist word for action is *kamma* (from Pali) or *karma* (from Sanskrit). At the root of karma is intention. When we apply the use of intention to be present and relieve pain in the other and ourselves, we engage with agency, our free will, and intention to act. In Buddhism, all actions, no matter how small, have consequences. Developing compassion and the intention to alleviate suffering can rescue us from sadness, helplessness, and the victory-less battle of trying to take away our child's pain. The Buddhist teaching of karma tells us we are responsible even for the thoughts we produce.

Longitudinal studies reveal that over time, parents with greater emotional balance and nonreactivity have children who also are better able to regulate their emotions.[11] Parents who feel confident in their abilities to parent and maintain agency—the belief that their actions have purpose and meaning—have a greater ability to be with difficulties. There is an extensive amount of research linking a child's emotional well-being with their parents' own emotional state.[12] When, as parents, we are caught in fear and anxiety, we transmit these emotions to our children. Calm parents make calm kids.

In My Life: It's hard to keep giving to my kids when my gifts are rejected. When I feel hurt, I can unconsciously protect or defend myself. In these moments, the last thing I want to do is be vulnerable or let them know I am hurting. This shared cycle of pain, protection, and hurt can play out unconsciously, taking us farther and farther apart. Sometimes it takes real humility and honesty to admit what I've been doing to try to feel safe. It takes empathy and compassion for all of us to begin to heal.

When Bella was in fifth grade and James in second, we went on a retreat to Blue Cliff Monastery, a practice center in the Plum Village tradition located in upstate New York. I had been taking my kids on Buddhist family retreats for a few years, so it wasn't a new thing, but my daughter was now at that age where being different or having a parent who was different was hugely embarrassing. Going to what felt like a family Buddhist summer camp was tipping into the way uncool category. Luckily for me, she had a friend, Ellie, who was up for making the trip with us. This friend of Bella's came prepared to combat the healthy monastic food, packing two bags of contraband Oreos, beef ramen, boxed chocolate milk, Count Chocula cereal, Cheetos, and gummy worms—all the food I was happy to leave behind. Ellie's mother wanted her to have this food: "Otherwise she just won't eat. She will go without, and then it's a real problem."

My husband does not follow a spiritual tradition; his temple is a walk in the woods or kayaking on a lake. But he is glad and supportive when I follow my chosen path. It benefits him as well: "You're a lot nicer now," he said after I'd been practicing for a few years. So, in the heat of August, I set off with three kids and two bags of food-like stuff for a week at the monastery.

We had roommates, another mom and her two kids. One of these children was potty training, and one was in kindergarten. Five kids in the room. The older children's first plan of action was to introduce the younger ones to their video games, which I limited to being played only in the room. The older children also introduced the younger to high-fructose corn syrup and the deliciousness of their contraband food bags. It was day three or four when I came back after the morning talk and meditation, around lunchtime, and saw the kids had not gone to the children's activities and had never left the room. Empty chocolate milk cartons, cookie crumbs, and packages of noodles were strewn about, and the kids were engrossed in a video game on Ellie's phone. They looked at me with sugar-glazed eyes as I stepped over the contents of their exploded backpacks. Wet towels were cleverly arranged amid empty cellophane packages, bright orange cheese crackers, and both clean and dirty clothing. The whole room felt like a soggy Petri dish about to sprout Lucky Charms marshmallows. "Do you see this room?" I asked. "It's full of trash and wet towels. I can't even walk to the bed. Look at all your stuff on the floor! Have you been outside today?"

"No, we ate in the room."

Clearly, they had eaten and not much else.

"We are sharing this room." I looked at the two younger kids and at my own son, now mainlining sugar and video games until he crashed out on the bed with the tweens. Why did I think the magic of the monastery had a chance against corn syrup and the animated flocks of vengeful cardinals jumping around in their video games? "I want this room cleaned up so we can walk through it. Get rid of the trash," I said. "There will be ants or mice if you don't."

I left in a huff, wondering why I brought them when they really didn't want to come. It wasn't working out the way I had hoped, and the kids I had brought were taking the two other children down with them. Even though the other mom took the corruption of her children very well and appreciated the attention the older girls gave to the little ones, it seemed like my kids weren't getting anything out of being here.

When I returned to the room, there was a note taped to the door. It was a picture of a heart, and when I unfolded the note I found an apology. Inside the room, the kids had folded their clothes and put them away. The wrappers were in the trash, and the floor was a floor again—space to walk on. The towels were in the bathroom and the kids were outside with the other little Buddhas, adventuring in the woods. Later that day, I thanked Ellie and Bella for doing such a thorough job, and I had some hope that the week could have some impact besides teaching them how to level up in *Angry Birds*.

The next morning, Bella sat next to me in the Great Dharma Hall. She leaned into me, and her whole body softened until she was lying in my lap. I stroked her forehead and rubbed her little girl shoulders with their tense muscles, the sharp bones so near the surface. She started to melt into the floor cushion, and she stayed in my lap with her eyes closed when her friend and her brother left with the children's groups. I used my thumbs to stroke the bands of muscles in her back and her neck, and my fingertips to brush her scalp and hair. I realized I couldn't remember the last time I had touched her, or she had wanted touch. She had stayed away the last few years, full of anger and increasing awareness of how uncool her mom was. And I had too. I was hurt by her withdrawal and had responded in kind to protect myself from rejection and disdain. I hadn't done anything except sneak a quick hug every once in a while.

When she was a baby, I would lay her down on a towel and rub her belly with oil, gently pushing in a circle clockwise to help with her colic. Even as a little girl, she would ask me to massage her. "Can you fix my back?" she'd ask me at night. Sitting there in the hall, feeling the softness of her body as she lay against me, I felt the joy of connection and deep regret that I had withheld touch to punish her for hurting me.

Things changed after the retreat, and for a while Bella was sweeter and more helpful. What stayed with me was the power of touch in our relationship. I resolved to deal with my own feelings and to take care of my own hurts. The intention to be a loving, compassionate presence includes ourselves. When our actions are born from compassion, we do not burn out because we are paying attention to our capacity. We do not overburden anyone we love, including ourselves. Compassion means first removing suffering from our own hearts and minds so we can do it for our children.

Even through the worst times we've had, when Bella was at her most angry and hostile, the ability to give her the gift of touch kept us somehow connected. It is still there: even as a big girl living away from home, she still wants touch. When I hear her say, "Can you massage my shoulders? They're killing me," I translate it to, "Please help me with my life." And I believe that touch does help, in a small way. It is a humble act of love and compassion—the ability to take away the pain of someone else, possible after we get out of our own way.

Mettā: Loving Kindness

Mettā, or loving kindness, is the path to compassion. Both loving kindness (mettā) and compassion (karuna) are included in Buddhism's four beautiful heart qualities, called the *brahmavihārās*. The Buddha gave instructions to his followers about cultivating these four states of loving kindness/universal friendliness (mettā), compassion/the wish to relieve suffering (karuna), sympathetic-appreciative joy (*mudita*), and equanimity-balance (*upekkhā*).[13]

The word *brahmavihārās* is also translated as "immeasurables." It signifies the highest realm of the heart and mind, a place where there is no hatred or dislike.[14] The word *brahma* in Pali refers to the god Brahma, who is without hatred. *Vihāra* means the dwelling places. The brahmavihārā qualities embody the highest and best homes of the heart and mind. The brahmavihārās are described beautifully by Akincano Marc Weber as "universal forms of empathy."[15]

Developing the heart qualities of the brahmavihārās, parents can learn to be balanced, loving, and compassionate in the midst of their child's pain. Our hearts can resonate with our child's and fully understand their suffering without being swallowed in it. Weber adds that there is "nothing particularly Buddhist about [the brahmavihārās]," as they are four mind-states that universally support harmonious and peaceful relationships.[16] These abodes reveal the natural goodness of humanity and remove any obstacles blocking the vast, fearlessly loving hearts we all possess.

Kindness, compassion, joy, and equanimity are ours from birth. We are spiritual and infinitely compassionate beings at our essence, when our hearts and minds are unclouded by anxiety, liberated from fear and judgment. When we practice mettā, we reconnect with the openhearted nondiscriminatory friendliness that includes all beings, including ourselves and our children. Mettā creates conditions for boundless love. It is love given freely, independent of what is received in return or how deserving someone seems. When such love encounters suffering, it naturally turns into compassion and sparks the intention to remove pain. When it encounters the good fortune of others and sees the beauty and goodness in them and ourselves, it is naturally joyful; we know this feeling from the way we celebrate when something wonderful happens to our kids—the happiness of others is our own happiness.

The Buddha instructed his disciples in the goodness of loving kindness practice and described it as a protection to ward off fear. He detailed eleven benefits for those who practice mettā. Such practitioners are loved by humans and nonhumans. They sleep easily and have good dreams. They are safe from assaults by fire, poison, and weapons. The heavenly deities look over them. Their minds are concentrated, and they have bright, radiant complexions. Finally, their minds will be clear at the time of death.[17]

While I cannot vouch for all of these benefits personally (in particular, I know nothing about the efficacy of a heavenly bodyguard), I do know that when I practice mettā, my view shifts from that of a small, rather helpless being in need of protection toward joining with something greater than myself. I connect with the force of love. When I send mettā to myself, I can move from worry and fear for my child to a place of abundant love that embraces any circumstance and degree of pain. Mettā gives me more perspective and solidity. It reminds me that love is greater than my pain; it is limitless.

Mettā meditation is also a way to become less fearful and biased. Instead of defending and protecting myself from attack or discord, when I open my heart to others and wish them freedom from suffering, I can connect with them. Including others in my prayer for well-being transforms them from strangers who are nothing like me to people who belong. They become people with tender feelings, just like me. The most interesting effect is that I also become harmless to them. This engenders a sense of safety, openness, and generosity that blossoms into a natural friendliness.

When love encounters wisdom, experience, and understanding, it becomes unshakable stability grounded in the knowledge that we can meet all situations with unyielding friendliness.[18] This is a place of flexibility, where parents can understand what is within their control and what isn't. Both knowing that suffering is natural and unavoidable and cultivating deep warmth and care make life better for ourselves and our children.

When my child was hospitalized, I would wake up at night with automatic thoughts of frustration and worry. What's going to happen today? Will she try to discharge herself? How receptive is she to treatment? Can I talk to the social worker? Will she comply with aftercare? All questions I couldn't answer, especially at 3 a.m. Lying awake, I used my mettā phrases for Bella and for myself: May you be safe and well; May you act with compassion for yourself; May you know you are loved; May you learn to care for yourself with ease; May you rest and know love is here. These words helped incline my mind away from the future and to a place of well-being and healing.

Dharma teacher Joanne Friday points out that the time we spend actively practicing mettā keeps our mind in a wholesome place and avoids the mind-states of hatred, hopelessness, and fear. The less time I spend in doubt and frustration, imagining the worst outcome, the more able I am to rest, nourish myself, and let go of the ever-present tension of believing my worry can actually save my daughter. This is the Third Noble Truth in action: there is a way out of suffering. I can let myself out of the prison of worry.

Mettā Meditation

Do your best to practice mettā for yourself at three intervals during the day. This could be on your commute to work, waiting in a checkout line, or while your coffee is brewing. The practice of remembering ourselves in mettā practice can help retrain our selective mind that forgets that we, too, as much as anyone, are deserving of love and care. When we actively remember to include ourselves in our circle of compassion and love, we can reverse the habit of abandonment and restore freshness to our minds and hearts, learning to trust in our own strength and friendship and to find our way back to balance, even when our child is suffering.

EXERCISE

Invitation to Practice Mettā for Someone Else

1. Calm and center yourself. Soften the area around your heart.
2. Bring to mind a loved one's face and body, possibly your child's; feel connection.
3. Offer them words that support. Some examples are: "May you be safe and well," "May you be strong and healthy in body and mind," "May you care for yourself with ease," "May you see your light," and "May you be fearless and free." Find three or four phrases that resonate with you.
4. Repeat these phrases slowly three times.

Expansion

Begin by sitting in a comfortable position with a straight back. Relax your shoulders while keeping your heart space open. Allow your belly to soften, and release any clenching or tightness in the stomach. Let your belly be the size it wants to be. If it feels helpful, close your eyes.

Take a few centering breaths and experience what it feels like to pause and invite stillness. On your exhales, cultivate the intention to release tension and soften the body, inviting a feeling of safety and harmlessness toward all beings.

When you have dropped inward and found your place of centered stillness, call to mind someone you find easy to love. This could be your child, an inspirational person, an animal, or a beloved friend or relative. If your child is your beloved, but thinking of them brings up feelings of grief or anxiety, for this exercise I recommend using an image and relationship that involves less complicated emotions. Since this practice is about cultivating the energy of loving kindness and having it manifest in the world, it is traditionally done with living beings, as they can receive the benefit of your energetic transmission.[19]

Bring someone you find easy to love to mind in detail: the way they walk, the shape of their body, and their expression. See them smiling, delighted to be in your presence. There may be a feeling of love or warmth, but it is perfectly fine if there is no overt feeling. This practice is to grow the willingness or intention to feel open and friendly.

Begin by wishing them safety and protection from accidents, then wish them to know kindness today. Wish them happiness, the ability to touch joy, and peace in the face of changing conditions. Invoke these intentions three times, and give space for any feelings to arise.

Repeat these intentions for yourself, offering the medicine you are wanting, solidity, wellness, or peace.

Continue by now offering phrases for a person you do not know well and don't have an opinion about, and lastly for an irritating person. Some days, both the beloved and the irritating person may be our child. Some days, you can be the irritating person.

It may feel forced and unnatural to wish good things to one who is making life feel difficult. It may be difficult to stretch to include this person, especially if there is fresh irritation or hurt. You may want to add "just like me" to the end of the phrases. Even in the face of difficulty we can wish, "May you know kindness, just like me." Lastly, send these wishes for happiness out toward the whole world, to all parents and children. We are all someone's child. Leaving no one out, encircle the globe with your capacity for caring and kindness.

In the classic form of mettā, after finding a sense of solidity, we start by generating loving kindness for ourselves. We then move toward a beloved benefactor, a friend, a stranger, someone who is challenging, and ultimately to the entire world. The prevalence of self-hatred and cultural conditioning in unworthiness in Western culture may make it difficult to begin with the self. In this case, it may be helpful to imagine yourself as an infant or to recognize your own innocence and gentleness by looking at a childhood photo. Practicing self-love is transformative. Being a presence of love reminds me that my intention to love no matter what is crucial for my kids.

In practicing mettā, find the phrases that are most alive for you. I find using the word *ease* gives me a scale to measure my effort against. When there is ease in me, life doesn't feel hard. When I track ease in my actions, I have a tool to notice fear and pressure. Lack of ease tells me I need to detach and seek care and support. You may need to adjust your phrases daily or even by the hour to find what really supports you right now.

Traditional phrases include:

May I (you, she/he/they, all beings) be happy, or: May I (you, she/he/they, all beings) be free from suffering and the roots of suffering.

May all beings be free from danger.

May all beings be free from mental suffering, or: May I be peaceful.

May all beings be free from physical suffering, or: May I be healthy.

May all beings have ease of well-being, or: May I be at ease.[20]

For some of us, words do not access our hearts, and we may just want to stay with the feeling that arises while contemplating a person we love. We can also access this heart space by cultivating a feeling of love based on an emotional connection independent of phrases, as the Buddha's original mettā teachings are recorded—simply radiate friendliness to all beings near and far. Allow this feeling of care and openness to permeate the mind and body. Does it have a color or a taste? Where is love in the body? Stay present with this feeling alive in you. Direct it toward yourself, to the best of your ability, and then radiate this feeling toward a neutral person, a somewhat difficult person, and finally toward all beings.

This training in universal, nondiscriminative friendliness can support parents encountering disappointment and fear about their kids' condition. The practice of mettā is also used as a means to develop generosity and social responsibility; it helps us to recognize, despite surface differences, that we will all encounter pain and we are all worthy of care.

May you be your heart's faithful friend.

May you realize the end of suffering in this lifetime.

May you trust your light.

CHAPTER EIGHT

Karma and Intention

Mind is the forerunner of all actions.
All deeds are led by mind, created by mind.
If one speaks or acts with a corrupt mind, suffering follows,
As the wheel follows the hoof of an ox pulling a cart.
Mind is the forerunner of all actions.
All deeds are led by mind, created by mind.
If one speaks or acts with a serene mind, happiness follows,
As surely as one's shadow.

    —*The Dhammapada*, TRANSLATED BY ANANDA MAITREYA

The word *karma* (in Sanskrit; in Pali: *kamma*) in common usage has come to mean a sort of secret reckoning tool akin to an omnipresent Santa Claus who knows if you are naughty or nice and rewards you accordingly. This is a distortion of the meaning of karma as the Buddha taught it. Karma means "action."[1] It includes the triple karma of our thoughts, speech, and bodily actions contained in the motivation of the action, the enactment, and the result. In Buddhism, we are responsible for what we think. We are responsible for how these thoughts make our words and our actions and what we contribute to the lives of our children.

The term *kamma-phala* means "karmic fruits."[2] I think of us all living as a vast interconnected web joined by millions of fine threads, and when I say, think, or do something, one of these fine threads vibrates and may break. We don't have the power to control the thoughts, words, or actions of others that cause the threads to slip around us. Everything is interconnected, even though we can't always see the full effects of actions. Karmic fruit is the result of the repetition of an action—including our looping thoughts. Karma shows up in our conditioned responses to situations and in the present moment. One way to see karma is to notice the present we create from our past, our biases, our training, and our internal voices. We can track generational trauma in ourselves and our children, especially if the trauma is nonverbal. Not acknowledging something can increase the potency and intensity of the trauma reaction. We can also see karma in inherited traits that pass from our parents through us and on to our children.

Recent findings related to neuroplasticity, the way the brain changes with use, support what the Buddha is recorded as saying 2,600 years ago: "Whatever a person frequently thinks and ponders upon, that will become the inclination of his mind."[3] The fruit of karmic conditioning unfolds in each thought, word, and deed we perform right now. What we think, say, and do matters in our own situation and in the lives of our children. Each action contains a seed of intention, which creates a feeling in the body or mind. Acting from fear or anger, for example, we experience distrust and aversion. Acting from the wish to help someone feel better, we experience a sense of connection and usefulness. This is the karmic fruit we experience right now—no need to wait until we are born into a future lifetime. Karma shows up in our exquisitely perceptive bodies and minds with each thought, word, and act.

The foundation of karma is intention. When we look at how we have been unskillful with our kids, we can consider why we acted the way we did. In all our acts are powerful motivators and protectors. All actions contain a beneficial intention that is a motivator; when we look deeply, we see all actions are in service of care for ourselves and others—even the painful ones.

The Buddha said that intention creates the foundation for the wholesome or unwholesome inheritance of our actions. Peace activist and Buddhist educator Donald Rothberg gives us his interpretation of the Buddha's words: "Intention, I tell you, is kamma. Having intended, one performs an action through body, speech, or mind."[4] This is good news, since it means that our intention and thought that precedes and conditions our actions is already an action.

It is intention that gives us back our agency and allows us to recognize that we are doing something of value. Let me say this again, because it's so simple and so contradictory: setting the intention to keep our heart open for our children and to stay solid despite the uncontrollable is already doing that. When I understand that my thoughts, prayers, and presence are an energetic creation, I see that they have a purpose and make a contribution. Living in alignment with our intention means we have already taken action. Aligning with our intention of compassionate support keeps us from experiencing helplessness or falling into despair and depression. This return to agency can shift the activation of the brain from a shared painful experience to one of soft joy at being a presence of care and support.[5] I can be present with my child in a way that aligns with my highest intentions and does not spill my suffering onto them.

Intention setting supports agency by creating clarity around how we want to contribute to the world. I think of intention setting as a profound gift I am committed to offering during my lifetime, to my children and to everyone I come into contact with. I see intention as a threefold form of care for myself, for my children, and for the world. To remember my intention, I've written it on my arm, my sneaker, and taped a note to my computer. It can be helpful to write your intention and have it in your pocket or wear a piece of jewelry that evokes your intention. I've considered getting a tattoo of my intention, but since it keeps shifting with my life circumstances, it seems I'd end up with a long grocery list on my arm. Impermanent ink suits my life better.

Buddhist scholar and monk Ṭhānissaro Bhikkhu calls attention to the Western saying that the road to hell is paved with good intentions. In Buddhism, he says, the road *out of hell* is paved with good intentions. Intention, or *cetana*, is linked to the inescapable inheritance of our actions. In his translation of the Five Remembrances, Thich Nhat Hanh writes, "My actions are my only true belongings. My actions are the ground on which I stand."[6] We cannot deny we have performed the actions that create our life. Buddhism values the intention behind our actions as the catalyst for the outcome.

In My Life: When my daughter was in fourth grade, we were not having a good year. She was angry at home and often lashed out verbally. Sometimes she was tearful and anxious. Her moods shifted quickly; often they were intense and stormy. Crying episodes lasted hours, and nothing I did offered her any comfort. On a recommendation from a spiritual friend, I took her to a therapist. It was a cold gray day in February, and Bella was angry about the appointment because it meant she was going to miss two hours of her friend's birthday sleepover. I had tried to shoehorn in both the therapist and the party to fit everyone's schedules; it wasn't perfect, but it was the best I could do. My son, James, was with us—he was around four, and, as usual, he went everywhere I did.

I reassured Bella that I'd have her to the party in time for dinner, but she was mad. Not a good start. She didn't want to sit near me or to talk at all during the session. James sat on my right side, playing with one of his matchbox cars. About twenty minutes into the session, while I was telling the therapist what life and Bella's challenges were like for me, Bella walked over and punched me on the shoulder. Hard.

I couldn't hold it together. I'd spent the last hours getting two kids in the car and dealing with Bella's resistance, and now embarrassment and shame that my daughter had just hit me in front of a stranger flooded over me. I started to cry. James curled closer to me and started stroking my arm, raising worried eyes to mine. The therapist looked at me crying and at James comforting me while Bella stood at a distance and said, "She doesn't treat you well. She just hit you." There was a pause as I continued to cry, harder now that the therapist had pointed out Bella's lack of consideration and respect—something I hadn't been prepared for. James was patting my hand softly. "Your daughter is nothing like you, and your son is exactly like you."

How do I parent a child who is nothing like me? How do I set boundaries for someone who responds with who responds in ways I find utterly unpredictable? How do I stay connected to someone I don't understand? The therapist recommended a book of parental discipline for strong-willed children; reading it made my stomach curl up into a knot. Setting limits, rules, and boundaries simply for the sake of teaching Bella to comply felt wrong to me. My heart told me this wouldn't work for either of us. This approach wouldn't honor my true motivation: it took me a while to figure it out, but what I wanted was consideration. I wanted respect, for both of us. I was part of this equation, and so was she. We both mattered. I couldn't do something that didn't align with my own value of compassion.

I recognized that I needed to parent my daughter in a way that felt authentic and aligned with my intention, and that my parenting would not look like other people's parenting. I didn't have a formula or a book that would give me the answers. I had my own awareness of my emotional life, and I had the intention to continue to be a presence of care and openheartedness for myself and my children as best I could. I had to feel my way along and check my own heart every step of the way.

Depending on the situation, staying with our intention may take different forms. I've learned to notice when I am in alignment and when I am moving into judgment or closing my heart. There are signals that I've left my intention of compassionate presence and need to reconnect with my own desire and what I can control: if I find myself feeling frustrated by my child or start having inner commentary about what they should or shouldn't have done, I know I need to pause. If I can't spend time with my child when they are suffering (which can express itself as anger, opposition, depression, or irritability) without these reactions, I know I need to care for myself. Doing so allows me to be calm enough to live in alignment with my intention to care for my children fully.

When I accompany my child and stay connected to my own experience of caring, I can find ease and faith that I am capable of showing up for all the situations in my life without preference. Acting out of fear and panic is a defensive reaction to what we see as intolerable. Beneath the scrambling fear is an unspoken certainty: we are not equipped to deal with this situation. We have disowned our capacity for wisdom and lost our confidence in our ability to handle what is unfolding. When I practice living in line with my intention, I often feel a tenderness I've come to associate with not abandoning myself. This tenderness has been a surprising development along the path of staying connected to my desire to embody compassion.

Intention inclines the mind in the direction I value. It is not a foolproof recipe for changing the situation. You may have heard the Buddhist phrase "nonattachment to outcome." This idea is counter-cultural in our results- and profit-oriented capitalistic society, where proceeds wash away any sins of our methods. Getting our way and getting the best results are what most of us think of as success. We may not have experienced how taking intentional steps throughout a process can be of greater value than any end product.

Acting with wholesome intention remembers the commitment to love, which supports the desire to remove suffering. Through the path of compassionate empathy and understanding the suffering of our child, we act with the intention to relieve pain. This desire creates a solidity and a nonpersonal resolve to be present. Acting with love and compassion imparts a profound purpose to our actions, and we learn that sitting with another and sharing their pain while not abandoning ourselves is a way to escape the fear and doubt that accompanies suffering.

If we are dealing with a condition in our child such as an illness or a mind-state, we know logically that we do not control the body or mind of another. Yet on some level, especially when this other is our child, we believe that if we try hard enough, research enough, and do the exact right thing that no one else has done, we can cure this, fix the situation, and take away their pain. But our child's path unfolds in accordance with natural laws. This does not mean what happens is welcome or just. It simply means that the vast interrelated history of life has brought forth this condition. This is karma.

Maria's Story

Sometimes we cannot make things change. It's a hard lesson of acceptance when we are confronted with situations where we can't take away our child's pain, no matter how hard we try. In Maria's story, we see how her intention to offer love supported an unfailingly compassionate presence that sustained her throughout unrelenting difficulty.

Maria has been a friend for over twenty years. She works at the city housing authority and uses mindful breathing at work to increase her capacity to stay compassionate with people who are often frustrated and angry. She asked me eight years ago to teach her son Jack some calming mindfulness practices. Jack was nineteen and had just been discharged from a psychiatric hospital. He was diagnosed with bipolar disorder and so heavily medicated that he couldn't chew solid food. Still, he paced the floor and wouldn't sleep for days. Maria was adopted and never knew her biological father. She was tormented by questions of where this illness had come from. No one in her maternal family or in her husband's family had bipolar disorder; how could this happen? There were no answers to the origins of these problems, and Maria's life felt out of control. She was in a constant state of worry and panic.

The doctors tried to find medication to regulate Jack's manic state, but the dosage was so high that he couldn't speak and drooled. His body shook, and he slurred his words. He wasn't the curious and bright teenager his family knew. Jack had to withdraw from college. As the months went by, Jack developed other symptoms and was diagnosed with type 1 diabetes. This added more medication and difficulty to his already heavy load of prescriptions and therapies.

With his bipolar in a manageable place, Jack was angry. He didn't accept that he had diabetes or bipolar. "I was so afraid that he would hurt himself," Maria shares. "He was so angry. He just wanted to be a normal kid, and it was so hard." Maria called the police when Jack went missing for two days without his insulin pump. She imagined him falling into a diabetic coma or dying. "He would drink milk shakes and eat ice cream, everything that was bad for him. He didn't believe that he was diabetic. His sugars would be five or six hundred. He wanted to hurt us. I was angry and scared and didn't know what to do."

After Jack experienced the consequences of not using his medication and was back, he began to regulate his blood sugar and take his insulin. He managed his blood-sugar levels and finished his second semester at college, but afterward, he had another manic episode. "He thought he was Batman. He would wear a cape and jump on things. He walked around and talked to people. He was very intrusive. Someone could have hurt him."

Maria couldn't keep her son safe or protect him from the chemical changes in his neurobiology that altered his way of relating to the world. Jack was again admitted to the psychiatric ward. This time, it was harder to regulate his medication. He was in the hospital for weeks. After his release, Jack returned to college to begin his sophomore year.

"He texted me that he didn't feel good, and I said it was probably the flu," Maria remembers ruefully. He didn't answer his phone. The next day, she called the health service at the college, fearing he was in a diabetic coma. The clinic doctor found Jack unconscious in his room. "I got a call from Providence Hospital's ER that Jack had meningococcal meningitis, and if I wanted to see him alive, I had to get there in two hours. I was in a panic. I just went, and when I saw him, his face was so huge and discolored he looked like a monster. I couldn't believe it." Jack was in the ICU for nine weeks. He was in the hospital for almost six months. The bacterial infection from meningitis caused necrosis. "He looked like he was burned from the waist down. Then the doctor told me they had to amputate his big toe to save his foot. It was so bad." Maria can hardly get the words out.

Maria and her husband kept a vigil at the hospital the next state over, two hours away, for over five months. They took turns visiting so that one of them was with their son every day.

"Something was giving me the strength. Love is so powerful; it makes you keep going. I look back and wonder how I did that. It was because he needed me; that motivated me. And I needed him. I had to be there. I had to be next to him. I knew my presence would make a difference. I remember when I would tell him I have to go back to work." Maria's voice breaks. "He would say, 'Don't go, Mom. I feel safe when you're here.' We didn't do anything, just sat there. It was only our presence. My husband's too." She is crying as she says, "Just there, loving him, just holding his hand. That's all."

Jack underwent seven surgeries in the hospital: six skin grafts and an amputation. After he recovered, he needed further surgery for the hammer toes and foot drop that resulted from nerve damage and amputation. He is a young man who won't swim or wear short sleeves or shorts because of the profound scarring on his body. As I write this, three years after his illness, Jack is scheduled for surgery on his good foot. If the surgery is unsuccessful, he faces a possible toe amputation.

Throughout this whole experience, Maria holds onto her intention to love without expectation. Through all the pain, she has learned the immeasurable value of her solidity and open heart. The intention to be a compassionate presence is felt. Even when we cannot change the situation, our intention can help us stay with our desire to care, and this can ease suffering for our children and ourselves.

Intention Setting

Intention setting can be a note we write to ourselves daily. This simple practice can help us stay afloat and give us back a sense of power over what we do have jurisdiction over. In my practice, I've written "May I be a presence of care for myself and others at each moment" on my forearm to have with me. This reminder created a deep shift in my experience from one that was full of thorns to moments of soft happiness as I recognized my capability to bring compassion to even the painful, disappointing, embarrassing, and unwanted moments. I experienced the joy of competency—knowing I could care for whatever arose, leaving nothing out.

Please try out some of these phrases. In my experience, there is a somatic connection, the unlocking of a stuck place in the body, when I find the intention that resonates with my true purpose. We feel the connection with words in the body, perhaps in a release of tension in the belly or a feeling of solidity and grounding. The wording of your intention is important. Allow your body to guide you when you try out these phrases.

EXERCISE

Invitation to Practice Intention-Setting Meditation

---

1. Calm and settle the body.
2. Come back to the breath, and rest with the inhale and exhale.
3. Ask what you are longing for right now, and then offer it to yourself. For example: "May I be calm and patient." "May I be solid and strong, even in this." "May I care for my pain." "May I risk opening to *x*, *y*, or *z*." "May I live without fear." "May I recognize what's good in my life." "May I see kindness in the world."
4. Ask what you want for yourself and your child, and then offer it to both of you. For example: "May I be a source of calm and love for you and me." "May I care for you and me." "May I know what is yours and what is mine to carry." "May I keep my heart open to you and to me."

Expansion

If possible, sit or stand silently. Allow the body to become still. Notice the contact points, the pressure of the feet on the floor, the weight of the body supported by the chair, and your hands in your lap or against your sides. Remember you are also this body. Notice the rise and fall of your chest and belly as your body breathes. Stay with the movement of the breath wherever it feels most alive, perhaps at the nostrils or the belly. Allow the breath to be as it is without trying to control or manipulate it. You may like to say silently, "This is how my breath is right now." Stay with the movement of the breath through inhalations and exhalations.

Then try out phrases of intention. Take your time. Attend to any signals in the body and mind.

Here are additional intentions you can explore: *May I meet all moments with kindness and love. May I not abandon myself. May I be there for myself. May I love and accept myself no matter what. May I be at ease with the changing conditions. May I remember my strength. May I be solid as a mountain. May I be open, balanced, and peaceful.*

My favorite intentions include: *May I care for me and for you. I love you. I am here for me. I am here for you. Let me respond with kindness and compassion at each moment. I care about this.*

Notice which phrases support you in this moment. If none feel just right, please make your own. Sometimes we need to make a new phrase every day or every hour to reflect our circumstances. When you find a phrase that aligns with your highest intention, return to this support often as a guiding star.

Grieving Ends the War within Ourselves

Grieving is a response to pain. To grieve is to let go of the images we've carried close to our heart, the mental snapshots in which our child is healthy, well, clean, sober, finishes school, or keeps a job. Grieving means we stay with ourselves through disappointment, heartbreak, or frustration. It allows us to feel the pain of our reality, to really understand how this situation impacts us, and to accompany ourselves. When we can hold grief and sorrowfulness, we don't run from our feelings. We make a nonpreferential container to attend to whatever is coming up.

If we truly grieve, we have more ability to be present when the waves get high. We know what to do. It might not happen quickly; grief is like a large pool feeding a stream. We can only shift some rocks to let grief flow out little by little. As grief leaves, space can open for the opposite of grief—the gratitude and happiness for what is still beautiful and delightful in life. The pool of grief can fill with a freshness as our care allows sadness to slowly ebb.

Willingness to be present with grief, fear, and anxiety in ourselves and our children is an example of stability. This compassionate response to the suffering of another is termed *anukampa*,[7] the Pali word for "a heart that trembles with the suffering of another." Resisting sorrowfulness may keep us safe from pain for a while, but it also keeps us far from the ability to accompany others.

Recognizing that our painful feelings exist is an opportunity to regard them as messengers. These unpleasant feelings of disappointment and wishing things were otherwise let us know we have conflicting desires—perhaps we want to stay home and care for our ill child but also desire to fulfill our obligations at work—or we long for something that is missing, such as understanding from our partner.

When we acknowledge that our values and intentions cannot manifest in this moment, we are able to grieve. Grieving means we give ourselves understanding and see the depth of our pain without becoming overwhelmed or consumed by it. We are allowed to grieve our unfulfilled wishes for a healthy child, our own inability to be present with pain, or the longing for a partner who has the capacity to listen without reacting. Grief can give us the emotional understanding and self-compassion that make it possible to move forward without resentment or anger. Grief allows us to stay true to our intentions for ourselves and our children. For more guidance on how to grieve, there is a detailed journaling practice on mourning in the practice addendum.

When we accompany ourselves, we do not lose ourselves in the undertow of feeling but instead stay rooted in the active intention to feel our pain without judgment or blame. We stop fighting against ourselves and simply acknowledge our heartbreak without needing to run from it. In this way, grieving and turning inward can help us move through deeply painful experiences with more resilience and capacity. This is the intention not to abandon ourselves, even in our deepest despair. As Thich Nhat Hanh says, "The way out is in."

CHAPTER NINE

The Peace of Equanimity

When my mind greets all moments with equal respect, it maintains stature enough to see that causal connections set every experience into its lawful time and place, that everything is always—breathtakingly—the only way it can be. My heart, resting in equanimity, can respond with compassion.

—SYLVIA BOORSTEIN, *Pay Attention, for Goodness' Sake: Practicing the Perfections of the Heart; the Buddhist Path of Kindness*

Equanimity is the heart of a balanced life. If it's that important, why isn't it the first chapter in this book? Because equanimity needs the support of everything we've explored. It needs your understanding and your lived experience to make it possible. Equanimity is earned, not learned. We arrive at equanimity when we can be with this earthly paradox of love and pain with an open heart. Equanimity helps you see a door where you saw only a wall.

The ability to accompany pain, to grieve, and to be present for what is unfolding with perspective and wisdom is the work of developing equanimity in parenting. Equanimity is not stoicism, nor is it the false front of apathy or indifference. It is the fearless inventory of all our hopes, dreams, clinging, and disappointment. Equanimity looks at mourning, at loss, at the unacceptable, at joy and at pleasure, at whatever is too big, too ugly, or too unwelcome, and sees it all with calm eyes of tenderness and wisdom. Equanimity does not judge any emotion or loss as too small or too unworthy. Equanimity never says, "What do you have to complain about? That other parent has a real struggle." Equanimity is the soft strength of mindfulness, universal love, fearlessness, and understanding.

Equanimity is made from the agency that believes what we do has purpose and matters. It's made from our intentions and from understanding the truth of suffering and the unavoidability of pain. It's made from knowing that everything changes, from the boundless heart qualities of love, compassion, and joy, and from the simple wisdom of taking care of ourselves—grandma knowledge. It's made from deep love for our kids, from our own pain, and from knowing that it's okay when both love and suffering are here. I like the definition of being in the middle of all things and seeing with calm eyes. This is so challenging when someone we love is in pain, especially our child. Moving toward this balance and calm is a process of integrating confidence in our ability to show up for ourselves and our child while understanding what is ours to change and what isn't.

When I first heard about equanimity, much like suffering I didn't think it applied to me personally. It seemed made for hermits and contemplatives living lives of prayer and silence, for people I imagined didn't have volatile, complicated relationships and who didn't have to deal with the frustrations and judgments of family, partners, and kids. The term *equanimity* sounded passive to me, reminiscent of some kind of pack animal holding all of life's detritus without complaint.

This, of course, was a very incomplete understanding of an equanimous quality of mind. I've learned that equanimity does not mean accepting endless burdens with stoic endurance, but rather releasing the heaviness of control and the frustration of wanting things to be different. It is not coldness, but a balanced, wise perspective that offers solidity and strength when we encounter suffering. Equanimity gives the foundation to help us stop running from what we perceive as unpleasant, undeserved, and frightening. It gives us confidence that we know what to do with suffering and tempers overwhelm and despair.

In its full realization, equanimity is the ability to stay balanced and centered with a loving heart—to maintain the desire to relieve suffering despite the flux of our lives. Equanimity is not an achievement or something we get to claim, but a fluid way we relate to our changing lives and the lives of our children.[1]

In My Life: When Bella, fifteen, was a resident on the psych ward after her first suicide attempt and James, eleven, was experiencing concussion symptoms, I used time alone in the car to mourn the life I wanted for my kids and me. I couldn't tell other parents about what was happening with my daughter because I didn't want her labeled suicidal, depressed, or unstable only to have these labels follow her for the rest of her high school life and beyond. I had an overwhelming secret and more pain than I could hold.

My practice saved me. Each day I sat and calmed my body and mind in meditation. I looked at my feelings; I understood that this was suffering and that suffering is part of life. I used my breath to anchor myself when I felt pulled into a sea of despair. Recognizing impermanence in the truth that nothing stays the same helped me see that even though things looked unchanging, they weren't.

The one place I could go to share my experience was the Sangha, the community of mindfulness practitioners I had known for a decade. In the Sangha I found acceptance and understanding—no unwanted attempts to fix my daughter or solve my unsolvable situation. One of my friends described the time his teenaged daughter left home and went missing. He said that when he heard someone saw her at a truck stop, he wanted to both "rescue her and murder her." It was so relatable. I got comfort from turning to people who knew the pain of having a child taking huge risks with their life.

Slowly, things got better. My son saw a pediatric neuropsychologist who, after an hour's conversation, said, "Nothing is wrong with you." She told me, "Stop taking him to doctors." His nystagmus, headaches, dizziness, and constricted breathing, it turned out, were from panic attacks and anxiety that he wouldn't get well. At the end of the same day, my son looked at me in wonder. "I don't have a headache," he said. It was the first time he had been free of pain in three months. By the end of that week, James was back at school full time. The consequences of missing months of school were momentarily brushed aside by my relief.

On the psych ward, Bella got to know a twelve-year-old boy who was hospitalized after his third suicide attempt. "He's so little," she said. "He looks like he's ten." She met other kids with multiple suicide attempts, kids who couldn't stop cutting themselves, and those who were sexually and physically abused or neglected. She met "this girl who ran away and lived behind the 7-Eleven, sleeping in a sleeping bag by the dumpster" for months before she was found by social services. Bella noticed that "I am the only one here who has two parents that are together." She started to see herself and her family with more perspective. Meeting these children, my daughter's awareness of the impersonal nature of suffering grew. She began to see that she wasn't alone in feeling pain and that no matter how good your life looks on the outside, no one gets out for free. I believe this understanding saved Bella's life.

Equanimity offers the ability to see beyond our small interactions to a larger view of the world. It has brought peace and understanding to my relationship with my children during immensely challenging times. In equanimity, I can offer loving and allowing—both for myself and my children. I can keep my heart open to their suffering and mine without trying to control life. Equanimity has saved me from the suffering of futile efforts to manage my children's lives, and it has given me the strength to accompany myself when the path is frightening and the cost of a misstep seems to be life or death.

In the constantly shifting busyness of being a parent, equanimity offers the stability to keep loving our children, to care for our own emotional well-being, and to avoid falling into panic and despair when we can't change what is happening. Many of us long to be that parent or person who has the ability to stay balanced despite the uncontrollable vicissitudes of life,[2] despite those I love being healthy or ill. I don't know if my daughter will relapse and be hospitalized again or, one day, take her life. Equanimity offers me a space of rest; I can be near this unwanted truth instead of pushing it away in fear. Equanimity is holding pain with an understanding and love bigger than the pain.

The Qualities of Equanimity

We notice the strength and centeredness of equanimity when we encounter it—the physician who can tell the bad news with compassion and nonflinching, the grandmother who learns of her child's death in a car accident without rage. It is the ability to stand in the middle of the unwanted and to know that we are capable of fully meeting this moment without grabbing hold of external strategies like drinking, eating, shopping, or drugging to distract and numb ourselves. This sort of even-mindedness is an advanced practice that disengages us from the innate evolutionary survival strategy of grasping at what is pleasant while retreating from what is painful or unwanted.[3] Equanimity is described as "a perfect, unshakable balance of mind, rooted in insight."[4]

The Buddha used two words for equanimity. The first is recorded in the Pali language as *uppekhā*, which contains the combination of the prefix "gazing on without disturbance" followed by "eye" or "see."[5] The second word used for equanimity is less well known: *tatramajjhattata*. Buddhist scholar and meditation teacher Gil Fronsdal explains that tatramajjhattata comprises *tatra* ("there" or "all things"), *majjha* ("middle"), and *tata* ("to stand" or "to pose").[6]

These two words, uppekhā and tatramajjhattata, give us the vision of staying balanced while aware of all that is unfolding around us. The Buddhist understanding of equanimity contains an openheartedness that is not selfish and reactive or dependent on circumstance. Thich Nhat Hanh lists equanimity as an essential ingredient of true love and defines equanimity as "nondiscrimination," a love that does not exclude any being.[7] Equanimity maintains an unwavering wish for all beings to be at ease without falling into despair when this doesn't happen.[8] I need to include all of myself in equanimity, my fear as well as my hope.

The Buddha's teaching of the Bamboo Acrobat illuminates this balance of caring for others while caring for ourselves. The story goes that a pair of acrobats—a master who was an older man and his assistant, a young girl—are practicing their craft. The master climbs a tall bamboo pole, and the young girl climbs up after him to stand on his shoulders.

The master tells his young assistant that in order to get down safely and earn their living, she should look out for him, and he will look out for her. The assistant, a young girl with very different ideas, tells the master that he should look out for himself, and she will look out for herself; that way, both will get down safely and earn their living.

The Buddha told his followers that the young girl had the right view.

Looking after yourself, you look after others; and looking after others, you look after yourself. And how do you look after others by looking after yourself? By development, cultivation, and practice of meditation. And how do you look after yourself by looking after others? By acceptance, harmlessness, love, and sympathy.⁹

The Buddha went on to emphasize that when we practice mindful meditation, we are taking care of others by attending to ourselves and our capacity. The acceptance, harmlessness, love, and sympathy we cultivate go in all directions. We offer these qualities to ourselves and to others. I recently heard a comment in a sutra study group that the young girl in the story sees the interconnected nature of caring for others through caring for ourselves by looking around from her high vantage point on top of the pole. Her posture reminded me of the two words for equanimity, uppekhā and tatramajjhattata—the ability to stand in the middle of things and look with clear and calm eyes. This is what we are called to do: become the best at nurturing ourselves so we can shine the light of support for our children. We bring that power to the relationship. We can be fierce protectors and advocates for both our child and ourselves.

Equanimity is also referred to as the "queen or king of the brahmavihārās,"¹⁰ as it gives the stability of wisdom to the other heart qualities. Each Buddhist brahmavihārā has a "near enemy" that resembles its state of openheartedness but leads us to a different destination. The near enemies are conditional: possessive love instead of mettā, pity instead of compassion, exuberance instead of sympathetic joy, and indifference or coldness instead of equanimity. These differ from the "far enemies," which are easy to spot: hatred, violence, jealousy, and reactivity.

Equanimity keeps our compassion from becoming pity, which looks down on the pain of others, and it keeps our joy from becoming forgetful exuberance that disregards the circumstances of those around us.[11] Just as each brahmavihārā requires equanimity, true equanimity is not possible without the other brahmavihārās. Universal friendliness (mettā) keeps equanimity from coolness and indifference—it stops us from kicking our child out of our heart when they do something we disapprove of. Compassion adds intention and action, and joy keeps equanimity from becoming tired and shallow.

Nonattachment to outcome is another aspect of equanimity.[12] If I have detachment from outcome, I am free to love fully without having my love be returned or justified. If my child is an addict, I can love them independent of them getting clean and sober. The word *detachment* can be confused with indifference or apathy.[13] Detachment is not apathy. Detachment means that we recognize we cannot control others—no matter how beneficial our intentions are. We do not control the cells in our children's bodies. We can't change their minds and make them think happy thoughts when they are depressed. We can't save them from their suffering. We can only actively work to create conditions that support their healing. One of the greatest supports for our children is our own emotional well-being, and *that*, we can do something about.

Equanimity Meditation

Kamala Masters, an Insight Meditation teacher and mother of four, leads retreats on cultivating equanimity.[14] She teaches that Buddhist equanimity practice, unlike the practice of mettā or loving kindness, which focuses on sending goodwill toward another, takes the self as the recipient. Equanimity is always for me to find balance. When I include my child in equanimity, I am sending intentions for balance and wisdom to myself in this relationship and in this world of ten thousand joys and sorrows.

In equanimity, parents can examine their relationship with their child while caring for their own emotional response.[15] The basic equanimity practice consists of holding thoughts of understanding and nonjudgment while acknowledging the truth of our limits and capacity.[16] Masters cites reactivity as the opposite of equanimity and offers the phrase "This is how it is right now" as a reminder that all situations, things, and beings are impermanent and changeable. Accepting one's emotions, mood, and circumstances, aware everything will change in spite of what we want, can act as a steadying anchor and free us from the prison of reactivity.[17]

Listening to your feelings as they unfold from moment to moment and showing up for yourself is a critical step to developing the present-moment awareness necessary for equanimity. Equanimity is an advanced practice to keep our hearts open to those we love when we feel hurt. It takes all of our wisdom and resolve to stay and care for the pain without tightening into judgment and distancing.

EXERCISE

Invitation to Practice Equanimity

EQUANIMITY FOR MYSELF

Take your space. Calm and center. Repeat these phrases silently to yourself:

1. May I know solidity. May I be peaceful. May I be steady and balanced in the face of change.
2. Even though I may not understand or like what is happening, things are unfolding according to a lawful nature.
3. May I hold my suffering with wisdom, patience, and balance. May my heart rest in love. No matter how much I want things to

be otherwise, they are as they are.

4. May I remain at ease in the middle of things. May I know peace even in this. May I accept things as they are right now. May my heart be open to my suffering. May I release my desire to control, and may I know that love is here.

5. May I have compassion for my own pain.

EQUANIMITY FOR MY CHILD

Take your space. Calm and center with breath or finding stillness in you. Repeat these phrases silently to yourself:

1. No matter what I wish for, things are as they are. May I hold your suffering with wisdom, patience, and balance.

2. May I keep my heart open to your suffering.

3. I love you, but I cannot save you from pain. May I be peaceful and balanced in the midst of this. May I recognize that this too will change. May I find calmness even with this.

4. May I see the world unfolding with quiet eyes. I soften the urge to fix and control. I hold you in my heart; may I love you in this moment.

5. (For an older child): I love you, but I cannot change you. You have your path and I have mine. I can care for you, but I cannot control your choices. Your happiness is based on your choices and not on what I wish for you. May my heart be steady and open to you.

Expansion

First, we sit with solidity and bring the mind to our own capacity for stillness. Recognizing our ability to connect with our own presence, we bring our awareness to the breath. We allow the back to support us while the chest and belly are open and undefended. We can let the belly be the size it wants to be and consciously relax the muscles in the armpits to soften the chest.

When we find calm and tranquil abiding, we begin silently repeating phrases, whether for a difficulty in ourselves or with our child. Equanimity always moves toward offering balance to ourselves. These phrases can be divided into those we use with a sick or injured child and those we use for someone who is older and capable of making their own choices. This might be a teenage child, a parent, a relative, or someone in a difficult relationship, suffering with an addiction or an illness because of their choices.

To begin working with a child or someone who is sick or injured, repeat the phrases that resonate with you silently to yourself. Stay with these wishes until you feel a softening in the body and receptivity in the mind. Then call to mind the one you care for and your specific situation. You can add these phrases to your meditation as you like: *Even though I may not understand or like what is happening, things are unfolding according to a lawful nature. May I recognize that this too will change. May I be at ease with the changing conditions. I love you but cannot keep you from suffering. No matter how much I want things to be otherwise, they are as they are. May I open to the changing conditions of my life. May I know peace even in this. May I release my desire to control.*

After coming into stillness, other phrases are suggested for working with a mature and reasonably healthy child/adult capable of making their own decisions. Remember to bring your attention to the body first and to consciously release any tension from your shoulders. Release protection and judgment from around the heart. Feel the rise and fall of the breath and the movement of the ribs. Let the stomach know you are safe and that you care about your emotions. When we sense a softness and receptivity in the body, we can begin. We can repeat silently: *May my heart be peaceful. You are the heir to your own karma. Your happiness and unhappiness depend on your actions, not on my wishes for you. I can care for you, but I cannot control your choices. May I keep my heart open to suffering. You have your path and I have mine. Right now, it's like this for you and me.*[18]

In equanimity, we have enough strength, wisdom, and love to allow all of our emotional states, all of our thoughts, fears, and joys, to be known. We do not discriminate. We have a tender, loving heart that will hurt when we encounter suffering in our children or those we care about. Equanimity is a way to extend love to ourselves and others. We do not withhold love because someone is in pain. When we love in a transactional way, their pain becomes our problem. Equanimity fills the well of care and compassion for ourselves so we are able to care for others.

Capacity

In order to develop equanimity as parents, we learn to stay with our child's distress and not try to push past this painful moment. With the support of mindfulness of feelings, we learn to investigate with curiosity and openness, without exceeding our capacity to stay balanced.[19] Awareness of capacity is key. Exceeding our capacity can cause strong reactivity and overwhelm. Meeting our experience with kindness and honestly assessing what is useful develops the courage and availability to be with more and more challenges. Just as a wise marathon runner trains by running smaller circuits to develop the muscles and aerobic capacity to go longer and longer distances without exhaustion, we train to meet all of our emotions without fear or disapproval. Becoming familiar with all emotional states and not rushing through or over them builds the muscles of nonpreference and the foundation of solidity.

Equanimity is linked to "cognitive flexibility," a principal element in the ability to care for stress and discomfort.[20] Dealing with children in distress or pain provokes powerful emotional reactions. Acknowledging and caring for these strong emotions in ourselves with equanimity promotes a faster return to balance than numbing, avoiding, or distracting. A panel of neuroscientists and psychologists focused on the benefits of meditation and mindfulness concluded that the qualities found in equanimity (resilience, agency, and an understanding of both impermanence and the impersonal nature of suffering) contain the most effective and important ingredients for well-being.[21] When we see success only as the end of suffering in our kids, it is easy to shut down and burn out if this doesn't happen. This group of investigators recommends cultivating the practice of equanimity as a method for improved ability to thrive in difficulty and stave off burnout.

Equanimity is an emotion regulation practice different from other strategies of cognitive or behavioral modification. Equanimity does not require effortful control.[22] This means that as we develop our capacity to stay centered in the midst of adversity, mature equanimity can become a trait rather than a temporary state. Equanimity can become part of who we are as people and as parents instead of simply a tool we pick up and put down. Using mindfulness of reactivity and an empathetic response to our own emotional state, parents can uncouple from automatic habit patterns that create more tension and anxiety. Over time, I can learn to maintain emotional independence and have some peace in the knowledge that my efforts are doing something, even if I can't see results right now. This ability to be with whatever is arising without being pushed and pulled by the worldly winds comes with experience.

Our stability is felt. Child anxiety researchers tested the theory that anxious parents who demonstrate rescuing and intrusive behavior impact their children's anxiety levels. A 2008 study measuring the speed of response time and anxiety levels in parents demonstrated that parents who had the least capacity to be with the recorded skit of a child in distress transmitted the same inability to be with discomfort in their children. Researchers discovered a direct correlation between the parent's and child's anxiety.[23] This means when someone else's pain stimulates more discomfort and intensified anxiety than you can bear, you pass this response on to your child. As my Dharma teacher says repeatedly, "What we do not transform, we transmit."

Through observational learning, children assimilate the non-verbal emotional attitude of their caregivers the same way I learned both to rage and to value spirituality from my parents. It wasn't their words; it was what they prioritized and how they acted.[24] Similarly, children who are in persistent pain experience increased physical pain, fear, and stress when they witness their caregivers in distress.[25] If I am anxious and distressed when my child is in pain, they will feel worse. Paradoxically, heroic attempts to intervene and save children from pain and suffering create fearful, anxious, less resilient children who have no faith in their emotional competence or ability to cope with pain and difficulty.[26] It is as if all our rescuing sends the message that these kids are not equipped to figure out life on their own. One of the best practices recommended by childhood anxiety researchers is for anxious parents to develop their own capacity to accept and tolerate discomfort in their children.[27]

This does not mean a phony stoicism. We're not assuming a "don't care" attitude or telling our kids to get over it. Any pretense is exactly that—pretend—and an attempt to bypass emotions teaches children how to ignore and abandon themselves. Learning to be fearless companions for our children requires that we let go of our fantasies about what their lives should look like, what qualities they are supposed to have, and any idea of fairness or entitlement. Thich Nhat Hanh often says hope can be an obstacle if it keeps us fixed on the future and prevents us from being present in our lives now. Releasing efforts to control, bargain, or even hope can bring us freedom—we are capable of meeting our life just as it is, with compassion, patience, and presence.

In My Life: Back in 2015, when my children's acute crisis phase ebbed—James's concussion had resolved and Bella was out of the hospital, seeing a therapist, and back in high school—I took a trip I'd always wanted to make. I went to Plum Village, a Buddhist meditation center in France founded by Thich Nhat Hanh. I knew this would be a good place for me to fall apart, supported by kind monastics who know how to be with suffering. For two weeks in Plum Village, I spent time doing slow walking meditation and reflecting. I waited for the suffering I hadn't dealt with to emerge. I waited for the unwept tears and the grief to flood me. I waited ... and I waited

... but the sorrow and despair never came. Where were the unfelt feelings, relentless fear, and dread?

It took days for me to realize: there was no residue left over. I had stayed with what was arising, had been present for myself, and there was no cache of pain hiding beneath the rug for me to deal with. There was sobriety and a deeper understanding of pain and suffering, but I was not sad. What I did notice when I returned home was a gentle determination, a consistency in my practice, and the ability to see beauty in the everyday and ordinary existence I would once have called boring. There was more joy in the ordinary, and I could see the gifts I had been given more clearly. My practice, which had supported me through the most difficult moments of my life, was one of these gifts.

As I work to develop equanimity in my life, I am increasingly able to notice when I am out of balance. This requires staying with my body and mind and paying attention to the signals of discomfort calling to me. If I power through and deny my emotional landscape, I can end up only recognizing signals once they cross over into distress, paralysis, or overwhelm. When I find myself judging my child, feeling overburdened or disrespected, or there's an urgency that won't let me look away, I can remember these signals are wake-up calls: I am needing care. With practice, I learn to stay present with the range of emotions in myself and my child with compassion and fearlessness.

Being with a Small Unpleasantness

Staying with actual sensation in the body is a way to understand the arising and falling away of emotions. This may be challenging for some of us. Culturally, we aren't taught to notice what's happening in the body in connection with difficult feelings. If we come from a legacy of abuse or trauma, it may not have been safe to feel into the body. Ignoring the body may have kept us able to function. Developing awareness and sensitivity to body signals can happen gently; only go as far as is comfortable. We never want to overload the nervous system and find ourselves panicking.

When we can expand our awareness and tolerate the body's expression of sensation, we quickly see that all emotions have a life span. This understanding of impermanence leads to comfort with changing landscapes of emotional, physical, and mental sensations as well as willingness to tolerate fluctuating mind-states without distancing and numbing.[28] Over time, we may become aware that the part of us observing agitation is not agitated. The part of us that knows we are overwhelmed is not overwhelmed.

For this exercise, you will need a clock and a comfortable, quiet place where you feel safe stopping to focus on your own experience.

EXERCISE

Invitation to Practice Five-Minute Distress Tolerance

---

1. Set a five-minute timer.
2. Take your space. Calm and center.
3. Recall a slightly painful experience. Choose a mildly stimulating situation—a small frustration or disappointment to work with. Keep it to an intensity of one or two out of ten.
4. Let go of the story, and focus on the body's reaction.
5. Locate the sensations in the body. Rate the intensity of your bodily reaction on a scale of one to ten.
6. Observe how bodily sensations change for five minutes.

Expansion

Locate where the sensations are most alive, and rate the level of intensity. Stay with this place of activation. Label the sensations, and continue to assess the level of intensity at one-minute intervals. Notice if the intensity increases or diminishes with attention. Notice any changes in bodily sensation. Notice what happens in the mind as the attention focuses on the bodily experience and drops the story. Did the initial perception about this experience shift at all? What changes occurred in the body and the mind? There are no right answers. This is an exercise to learn what supports your ability to be present with strong emotions.

CHAPTER TEN

Riding the Waves

The whole spiritual journey is a continuous act of falling on our faces. And we get up and brush ourselves off and get on with it. If we were perfect, we wouldn't even go on a journey. We can't be afraid of making errors.

—RAM DASS, *Grist for the Mill: Awakening to Oneness*

In My Life: A few years ago, I took my two children to the West Coast to visit the college my daughter planned to attend in the fall. After eight days of intense togetherness, including the three of us sleeping in the same room, we were all feeling strained. My daughter's reactivity was triggered by a series of small disappointments, including that the food was different. Bella expressed her anxiety and frustration by refusing to eat until she was back in Connecticut. She spent time sobbing in the bathroom and became so agitated that she bolted from our hotel with the intention of hitchhiking two hours to the airport and staying there until we flew out the following day. I was aware that my support system was absent. My friends, my partner, and my Sangha were all on the East Coast. I tried to use the phone and texting for support, but ultimately, I was alone to deal with this situation.

Bella was over eighteen, and I knew I couldn't legally stop her. I felt helpless and confused and didn't know how to help her. I was afraid she was going to be picked up on the highway and hurt or sexually molested. She did return to the hotel that day, but the level of emotional upheaval was huge. She also needed me to drive her to a walk-in clinic and wait with her to treat a chemical burn from a do-it-yourself eyelash perm gone awry.

The next day, I did not have the capacity to respond with patience and calm. The borrowed car was due to be returned to its owner in two hours. We had cleaned it out and were taking pains to keep it pristine. When Bella presented herself to be driven to the airport with a brimming cup of tea minus a lid, my own need for respect and consideration rose up. I kicked over the cup of tea. As I walked to the trash with the empty cup I yelled, "I am still your fucking mother!" Returning to the car, I recalled that in a few months I would be teaching a workshop on equanimity for caregivers. I hoped no one was filming me.

We pulled out of the parking lot, and as I drove, I remembered my deepest intention: to be a presence of care for my daughter and myself. I said, "I am really disappointed that I yelled at you. I want to show consideration and respect to us both. Can you tell me how it was for you?" She didn't answer, but I knew she heard my regret even if she wasn't ready to talk. We teach what we need to learn, and I know that parenting is my classroom for developing equanimity.

When I got home, I was disappointed that I had fallen so far off-center. I could feel how unbalanced I still was, physically and emotionally. I saw that my actions came from a deep desire to care for myself and to keep my children safe. I also had the desire to fulfill my responsibilities to the car owner and understood that I had been in sore need of some support at that moment. I recognized that, due to the emotional intensity of the trip, my reserve of patience and stability had been deep into the red.

Equanimity is sometimes likened to riding a surfboard—you learn to relax and stay balanced with the rolling current without clenching or gripping. As parents and human beings, sometimes we lose this ability. We fall out of balance and may end up shocked and disappointed that our actions did not support our intention to be a presence of love and care for others and ourselves. We may not only fall off the board, but find ourselves washed up on the shore with no board in sight.

Acknowledging these moments and mourning the unkind or unhelpful things we did or said is part of learning to keep our footing.

Balance

When we are balanced, we know it. An internal guide gauges how I am in this moment. As when balancing scales, the quality of care must remain carefully distributed between ourselves and others to avoid tipping into despair, helplessness, or fear. It's really algebra: what goes out as care to our child on one side of the equation must be added to our self-care on the other side so that the two sides of caring balance. This balance of care must be sensed and attended to for us to be in equilibrium. Care requires a somatic, embodied awareness that lets us know when we are losing our steadiness and tipping into reactivity.

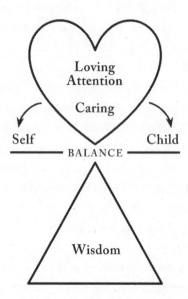

The balance between self and child rests on the fulcrum of wisdom. When we are aware of our own mental state and offer compassionate presence to ourselves in times of instability, we create the first level of balance. To do so, parents can rely on an understanding and experience of the truth of existence—that the only thing we can control is our response to life. This truth may challenge beliefs and desires about what we think is acceptable for our children. Wisdom contains acceptance, nonreactivity, an understanding of karma, suffering, and patience grounded in nonattachment. Wisdom is not intellectual knowledge, but the lived experience of how suffering can be transformed through practice.

If my child is having a panic attack and acting impulsively, I become afraid that she will harm herself. If I extend 70 percent of my care reserves and stability to her, I need to replenish these later to maintain balance. If I was only at 20 percent when the episode began, I am sorely in need of care and nourishment for myself. If I continue to attend to my child despite how depleted I am, I will pay for it. I may become sick myself. I may have my own angry outburst and become enraged at my powerlessness. My lack of resources may show up as depression. Maybe I will become emotionally fragile, doubt everything I do, or become paralyzed. These are all signals that the caring needs to flow in again before it can flow out. I've experienced relief hearing this reminder from meditation teacher and psychologist Akincano Marc Weber: "My needs do not go away because your needs seem to be bigger."[1] The adage "You can't give what you don't have" holds true.

The work I do in the residential teen treatment center is focused on reacquainting these teens with their true nature by shining a light on the lovable and loving hearts they all possess. I ask myself often in the work I do, *Where is the love right now?* as I navigate my own ability to extend loving care. Sometimes, when I feel rocked by rejection, hear harsh words, or experience actions that push me away, the love needs to move toward me. Sometimes the love flows easily between us, and the teens I work with see how their beautiful heart qualities are a gift to themselves and others.

After returning from my college trip with Bella, I searched in my lexicon of practices for something that could remind me what it feels like to be a balanced person with the capacity to love myself and others. Knowing imbalance, I asked, *What does it feel like to be in a balanced body?* The body and the mind are one. Thich Nhat Hanh tells us when we want to bring peace to the mind, the simplest way is to begin with the body.

EXERCISE

Invitation to Practice Regaining Balance

Take your space. Calm and center. Repeat these phrases silently to yourself:

1. Aware of my body: I care about this body. Let me care for the pain in my body. May this body rest in this care.
2. Aware of my heart: I care about this heart. Let me care for the pain in my heart. May my heart rest in this care.
3. Aware of my child: I care for you but cannot keep you from feeling pain. May you rest in this care.
4. May I accept that your path is your own. May I be solid and balanced even in this.

Expansion

Accessing the pelvic floor, our emotional seat, can bring the felt experience of stability into the body. Sitting either cross-legged on a cushion or in a chair, allow the knees to be wide to open the pelvis. Do not be shy or modest about taking your space. Inhaling, visualize the breath drawn up from the core of the earth through the pelvis. Draw the breath into the body through the stability of the pelvic floor and exhale into the earth through the base of the pelvis. Continue breathing. With each exhale, imagine the body sinking into the earth, rooting into the ground like a tree and finding strength in connection with the solidity of the earth.

When there is a degree of stillness and solidity, begin offering phrases that give the care you need right now. Here are some possibilities, adapted from guiding Insight Meditation teacher Mark Nunberg's compassion and equanimity practice: *Beginning with the body, I extend my care to this body. I care about this body, and I cannot keep you from feeling pain. I care enough to feel whatever is here to feel. I know that I cannot control the circumstances of my life. I will touch pain and joy. Let me love this tender body without running from my pain. It is perfectly natural to feel pain. May my body rest in my own care. I know this caring heart. My heart has accompanied me through all my joys and sorrows. I send my care to this sensitive heart that is moved by the pain and suffering in the world. I cannot save my heart from hurt. It is natural to feel hurt. I care about this heart that hurts. I am not afraid to feel what I feel. May my heart be at ease no matter the conditions. May my heart rest in my care. May wisdom and love protect this heart always.*[2]

Extending these phrases to our child reminds us that we have the capability to extend love. Sharing our care lets us see who we really are and gives a glimpse of our true potential to radiate compassion. Bringing my child to mind, I say, "I care about [name], even though I can't protect you from pain. I care enough to be close to your pain. I cannot control the joys and sorrows in your life."[3] My caring has value. May you rest in my care. May I be at ease with change and find joy in its midst. May I be as solid as a mountain. May I accept that you need to learn in your own way.

In My Life: A few winters past, James was missing high school due to stomach pain. At first we thought it was a virus, but after weeks he wasn't improving. On the advice of our general practitioner, I booked an appointment with a pediatric gastroenterologist. Where I live, these specialists are rare. The first appointment I could get was for three weeks away at 8:30 a.m. on a weekday in Hartford, Connecticut. I consulted my maps app, which told me the office was thirty-four miles from home. To be safe, I estimated an hour's drive.

The day finally came for our appointment. As we got into the car, I opened my app and saw the estimated travel time was an hour and a half. How could that be? I found out why as I sat and waited in the line of cars while the traffic light turned red for the third time. I was aware of the burn of adrenalin in my forearms and an infusion of frustration and anger. I felt absolutely helpless in this traffic. I couldn't turn around—I was stuck with no possibility of escape. When I phoned the doctor's office, I was funneled into an automated voice mail system. "Please leave your name and a call back number," did nothing to comfort me, and I longed for another human to reassure me that my son would still be seen even when we showed up late. I had failed my son and was furious with myself. Why hadn't I checked the night before? Why hadn't I asked someone or known better?

I did my best to breathe and to remember my intention to be a presence of care at each moment, but my mind was churning. I wanted to be airlifted above this clogged morning commute and escape. The pain of my judgment and the physical sensations of helplessness and panic were making my trip a hell realm. *This feels terrible; I don't know what to do*, I told myself. In that moment I remembered tonglen.

The Tibetan practice of *tonglen*, or sending and taking, incorporates the understanding of our universally shared pain, the impersonal nature of suffering, and impermanence. I've relied on this practice throughout the years when things get really tough. Tonglen is especially useful because you can practice it on the spot in an emergency (or what feels like an emergency).

Once I remembered tonglen, I breathed in all the tension in my body and mind, felt the crunch of expectation and disappointment, and breathed out the wish for ease and spaciousness. I breathed in again and felt the helplessness, the fear that I was going to miss this appointment, the doubt that I would be able to care for my son, the binding frustration of being held in this line of traffic, and breathed out understanding for the situation, tender recognition that I care, and forgiveness for what I didn't know. Then I widened my practice to include all the people in this world of eight billion who, just like me, felt frustrated and blamed themselves. I breathed in with all the parents who were afraid that they couldn't relieve their child's suffering and felt the shared anger, disappointment, and feelings of hopelessness. I breathed out a breath of deep peace for all these people caught, just as I was, in situations we could not control. Breathing in, I took in our shared pain, and with each out breath I sent us all the wish for the capacity to bear discomfort and disappointment.

Practicing tonglen, I became the witness to my experience as well as the one who was in it. I knew that even though this moment felt out of control and uncomfortable, it was a moment of shared reality, and I was capable of transforming my emotions, no matter how fierce or unwanted. After practicing for a few minutes, I willingly breathed in the feeling of anger, hopelessness, and despair so others would not have to feel these things. Taking on their suffering and transforming it, I breathed out and sent all those feeling panicked at their lateness peace, contentment, and nonfear.

Tonglen isn't a magic bullet, but it can transform our understanding of a situation and bring compassion to our actions. When we breathe in and recognize all those we share this moment with, we are no longer alone or helpless. We become agents of our own well-being and active participants in the well-being of all those on this planet who are caught, just as we are. Practicing tonglen, I recognized that maybe I would have to reschedule, but it wasn't the crisis I was manufacturing. That day, we were forty minutes late and we still got to see the doctor. I had gratitude for the understanding staff and for the practice of tonglen that helped me transform pain and open my heart to shared suffering.

You don't have to have a crisis to start this practice. tonglen is as accessible as an inhale and an exhale. It can join us to all beings around the world, reestablish our sovereignty, and reconnect us with our true intention to live with kindness for ourselves and others. Though I practiced tonglen in a moment of suffering, it is also available as a practice to experience the joy of generosity when we encounter good things in our lives. When we experience a moment of peace and ease, when we have good news about the well-being of our child, we can breathe in the feeling of contentment and joy and offer it to all others we know who are suffering with similar difficulties. We can imagine all parents receiving news that their children are well and healed. In this way, we can bring meaning and purpose to what can be an intensely subjective experience.

This is the part of tonglen I often forget to do. I am so relieved when my drama ends, I forget that I am experiencing the ending of suffering. Thich Nhat Hanh talks about noticing the non-toothache and celebrating when your tooth stops hurting. This is the ability to take in what is going well, to cultivate this awareness in ourselves and be able to offer it as a gift to others. Staying with the end of suffering is hard for me—I tend to lean into the future, waiting for the next drama, and letting myself rest in happiness can be scary. Celebrating with myself and with others is something that takes reeducation in a world that has taught me to be vigilant.

Tonglen

The practice of tonglen moves us from victimhood and the isolation of personal suffering to connect us to all who are experiencing pain, just like us. Tonglen reminds us of the impersonal nature of suffering and develops compassion and *bodhicitta*—our Buddha nature of an awakened, loving heart. The practice of tonglen is simple; it recognizes our pain and the pain of others. Breathing in, we experience our discomfort, noticing the feeling, color, taste, and particulars of that suffering. Breathing out, we offer an antidote.

In formal practice, it is recommended to have meditation experience and the ability to be present with strong emotions, as tonglen can release feelings we may have tried to keep bottled up. For this reason, we can begin and end tonglen practice with calming (shamatha) meditation.[4]

EXERCISE

Invitation to Practice Tonglen

---

1. Take your space. Calm and center.
2. Notice discomfort.
3. With the inhale, breathe in any suffering: anxiety, craving, worry, anger, or jealousy. If it is small, cramped, or dark, feel that.
4. With the exhale, breathe out the antidote: calm, peace, love, ease, joy. Feel the space, light, openness, and freedom of this.
5. In this world of eight billion, how many feel the same as me and also suffer right now? Breathe in the shared pain of parents around the world experiencing similar circumstances. Breathe out freedom and ease for all of us.

Expansion

Calm and center your body. Find an anchor, either breath or the sensations of the body sitting or standing.

1. Notice discomfort. Breathing in, visualize this discomfort as heat, oppressive smoky air, and the colors red and black. We can feel unpleasantness as constriction and tightness, as if we are in a claustrophobic box. Breathing out, visualize brightness, pure light, space, and coolness. Exhaling, create the felt sense of the opposite of suffering. This is the first level of practice: present awareness of our suffering.
2. Recognize that in this vast world, there must be a few others feeling what we are feeling right now—boredom, ill health, grief, fear, or rage. Recognize the existence of these emotions in others and breathe in with all those, who, just like me, are suffering. Breathe out, offering space, coolness, and relief to myself and all those who, just like me, are suffering in this moment. This is the

second phase of practice: sending and receiving. Perhaps you too will find it easier to awaken compassion if you begin by sending it first to others and then include yourself.

3. Continue to breathe in the suffering of others—their panic, despair, or the obstacles they face—and feel it in the body and mind as cramped discomfort, constriction, anxiety, or pain. Breathing out, continue to offer light, freedom, ease, brightness, spaciousness, and the vast openness of the sky. Willingly breathe in pain and transform it with your exhale, knowing that you can be with suffering.

4. Return for as long as you like to your anchor, either breath or the sensations of the body sitting or standing.

This practice of tonglen is an embodiment of the bodhisattva path, which vows to alleviate all suffering in support of the awakening of all beings. Tonglen gives meaning to our suffering by changing it from a personal hell realm into a way to connect with others and transform the shared pain of living on earth and parenting a child through storms. Tonglen is a concrete act that manifests the intention of alleviating suffering in the world.

Pema Chödrön sums up the practice: "The very essence of the Tonglen outlook: when things are pleasant, think of others; when things are painful, think of others."[5] There is power in understanding our shared emotional states. When we open to the interconnected nature of our experience, our emotions no longer keep us isolated and reactive but transcend the personal and join us to countless others.

Coda

Watching the moon
at midnight,
solitary, mid-sky,
I knew myself completely,
no part left out.

—Izumi Shikibu

In My Life: Parenting my children, I've learned that the medicine I need changes. Living with a child with sustained mental health challenges, my ability to inhabit my life has increased with practice. And the struggle continues—it is never the same situation twice. Everything is changing, in and around me. What remains constant is that my child's pain is always calling me into a new relationship with my highest intentions. The difficulties I encounter continually smooth the rough edges of my heart and mind, giving me more wisdom, balance, and capacity as long as I have the courage to be near the pain.

It's been a while since I began writing this book. Now more than seven years after that difficult year when both of my kids needed so much, a lot has changed. My children have grown up. James is fully recovered. His injury left residue, though: when he went back to school after three months away, there was a large gap in learning. This led to self-doubt about his abilities. We enrolled him in a school for children with learning differences, and there he began to see himself as capable and smart. He is currently at a mainstream college and has experienced more trust in his ability to learn. Because of his experience, he has more compassion for kids going through hard things. And he carries an abiding dislike of doctor appointments.

Bella's difficulties continue to peak and fall depending on events and circumstances. She's been hospitalized two more times—four years ago, she made a second suicide attempt, and just this past month she was hospitalized for suicidal ideation and intention. In the hospital my daughter received a new diagnosis and now is on different medication. My wish for her is that she will continue to get support that allows her compassion for herself to grow. I know I am powerless to change her mind and to make her value her life. In my powerlessness, I turn to my own ability to respond to what is mine: I keep my promise to care for myself and my children, moment by moment, with compassion and understanding. Living with this intention, I can rest—even in the not knowing.

If I lift my eyes from my computer screen and look across my desk, I see a Japanese print given to me by my father. The print is of a warrior without armor. In his raised right hand, he holds a long wooden staff, which protects him from the flurry of arrows and swords flying at him from all directions. The warrior holds a long sword in his other hand, and he's running fast into this conflict. Some days I look at this man in the hailstorm of projectiles and say, "Yeah, this is exactly what it feels like." It can seem like there are problems in every direction. Bella, who now lives a six-hour plane ride away, is unhappy and starting to feel depressed and suicidal. The dog needs ACL surgery, kids at my work don't want to listen, there's no oat milk for coffee, my son lost his wallet, and the cat keeps throwing up. I see these arrows coming at me, and I see this samurai warrior with his fierceness and strength, running barefoot into the fray, so unafraid. I think, *You have real arrows. I have possibilities and cat vomit.* I've learned to ask myself, *What's the best thing I can do for you right now?* I know that all lotuses come from mud.

Patience, the Unpopular Virtue

When my kids are in pain, the last thing I want to be is patient. I want things to change now. I want the suffering to end. I've learned when I push too much too fast, I add more pain by designating this condition as intolerable and unacceptable. Labeling something as unacceptable is one definition of suffering. With such a label, I now have not only the painful situation, but also a second arrow of anguish in the form of my own intolerance.

The Buddha spoke of patience as the highest virtue we can cultivate. Patience is a necessary ingredient in the creation of equanimity and the power to stay the course. In our Western culture, patience is not a popular trait. It doesn't look like a virtue or strength. If we are patient, we are often seen as weak or passive. Our culture rewards those who make things happen and create change. We do not look favorably on patience. In most areas of life, patience is not only suspect, but actively discouraged.

A few years ago, a friend on retreat shared an insight about patience with a friend who was struggling with addiction. I loved it so much that he wrote it out for me, and I put it next to my bed: "Even on the same tree, all the flowers do not bloom at once." My parenting journey does not look like anyone else's, and I cannot expect theirs to resemble mine. I am progressing in accord with my own karma—not someone else's expectations—just as my children are.

We know what it feels like to try all the time and still feel like nothing turns out right. Patience knows even if things look stagnant, there is movement and change. Patience honors the pace of life and allows the natural order to unfold in its own time, even if it's not at the pace we want. This is the type of patience Dharma teacher Joanne Friday calls "gentle diligence over time." It is patience that allows us to move forward with joy instead of pain. It is not a flaccid, helpless acceptance, but one that can shift our awareness from conflict and oppression to dynamic capability.

Recently, I found myself in a classic triangle: parental anger, a hurt and unhappy child, and myself as the peacemaker. With understanding,

I could speak to the angry parent's deepest desire to keep their child safe and also recognize the child's wish for consideration and trust. In recognizing the positive intent of both parties, the strategies that brought forth conflict and hurt became obvious.

I did not have to fix the situation, but to give both parent and child empathy and understanding. I trusted their own wisdom to reconcile. It felt liberating to trust others and allow them their own process without forcing a resolution or rushing in to fix an uncomfortable situation. Patience allowed me to love both parties without making one wrong or judging them. Staying present for ourselves in the midst of confusion, discomfort, and the messiness of an unsolved conflict gives others the gift of trust in their abilities, authentic path, and process. This is patience.

I Matter

One of the most useful lessons I've learned is that what I do and how I am matters. Even when things are happening that I do not like or want, I have a choice in how I respond. My life and happiness are worth investing in. My actions, thoughts, and words with my child are meaningful, even if I can't see their effect right now. The quality of my consciousness is hugely important for my own balance and affects my connection with my children. I lean heavily on my intentions and keep them centered in my life.

I also use present-moment awareness to help me stay with what is and not fall down the rabbit hole of the future. Creating a small window of attention gives a framework for attending to the present moment. We can make the circle of noticing an hour, ten minutes, or ten breaths, whatever gives us the support and focus we are looking for. If we are very distracted, we may need to make a very small window, perhaps committing to staying present with this task for the next three breaths. Sometimes, that is all I can do.

As parents and as people, we are unique. No single strategy or technique can fit all of us. I've offered you a road map with healing stops along the way. We can heal the edges of pain and work toward the marrow of our being with the firm intention to sustain love for ourselves and our children, whether they get a splinter or something unthinkable happens. We have the ability to stretch our own compassion and wisdom to hold it all, even what we don't want. The practices in this book are for you to try out. Only you will know if they truly support you on your parenting journey. My hope is that these words can accompany those on a path of staying present with themselves and learning how to be as wide as the sky, big enough to hold everything.

I send my heart to your heart and wish for you to be a presence of care for yourself in each moment. May your heart be at peace in the midst of your life and may you rest in understanding and balance always. May this be so for you.

To live in the world with your heart undisturbed by the world, with all sorrows ended, dwelling in peace—this is the greatest happiness. For he or she who accomplishes this, unvanquished wherever she goes, always they are safe and happy—happiness lives within oneself.[1]

Practice Addendum

Mourning in the Moment

Mourning happens when a relationship changes. It is not confined to death or big losses. I can mourn the loss of ease in my life when my child gets sick or mourn that my idea of a simple life feels so far away today. The more I recognize changing relationships and mourn moment-by-moment dukkha, the better I can accompany myself through my life. In my experience, finding clarity about the impact of the loss and recognizing what matters or what I fear helps me to hold pain with more spaciousness and compassion. Depression can result from incomplete mourning. When we are paralyzed by grief, we can become helpless and despondent. Mourning in the moment gives us a way to continually process the small and big losses, separations, and disappointments we all face. The skill of mourning makes space for the other side of mourning, which is celebration. When we know how to mourn, we also know how to love better. This practice is adapted from Shantigarbha Warren, a trainer at the Center for Nonviolent Communication.

EXERCISE

Invitation to Practice Mourning My Relationship
with My Child

This is a journaling exercise. Find a quiet place where you can focus. Calm and center the body either by staying with the breath or inviting relaxation into the body. When you feel some stillness, begin by reading the following questions and giving yourself five minutes to answer each.

1. Bring to mind what's happening with your child. Tell the story to yourself. List any issues or judgments you have about it. Is anyone at fault? Do you blame yourself, them, or someone else? Write your feelings about having judgments or blame. Are you judging yourself for your judging? Just notice and name what's here. You don't have to fix or solve anything.

2. What was the moment you felt the loss connected with these circumstances? What did you see? What did you hear? Was it an internal message, or a sudden understanding? Were people with you or were you alone? Take time to recall the scene with clarity and record your thoughts.

3. How did you feel when you noticed this loss? Take your time to be with the feelings. Write the names of the emotions—whatever is true for you, no censoring.

4. Check in with the body and area around the heart. Look for heaviness, tension, or sadness. Take time to notice bodily sensations, and stay present with them, simply accompanying. Is there movement in the sensations? Do they get more intense, or less? Do they shift as you tune into them? Offer yourself patience and tenderness. Make a note of what you feel.

5. What is the significance of the loss? List the deeply important needs or values around it. What does it mean for you? Is it a loss of hope or dreams of health? Is it a loss of a way of relating to the

world or of a certain relationship with your child? Is it the loss of security that comes from living with a serious illness? Record your thoughts with a sense of honoring.

7. Notice how you feel now. Is there a shift in the quality of feeling or a different feeling? How is the body? Is there any change in sensation? Make a note of what is true for you.

8. Imagine taking a next step. What step could honor the significance of the loss? Possibilities include simple recognition, a conversation, creating a mourning circle, or sharing about this loss. You could also create a personal ritual or a sacred space where you place a symbol of how this loss affects you—something as simple as a flower before a photograph of your child, a smooth pebble in your pocket, a poem, or a letter that speaks of how this loss has changed you.

9. Write down what your next step will be.

EXERCISE

Invitation to Practice Awareness of Vicissitudes for Yourself

---

This is a wonderful practice to cultivate awareness of what is happening and see through any clinging to the pleasant or pushing away of the unwanted.

1. Calm and center the body.

2. What is causing pain in your life right now? Is it work, relationships, or something else?

3. Has it always been like this? Has it been better or worse?

4. What is going well in your life right now? What is making you happy?

5. Was it always like this, or has it changed? Do the same things make you happy as a year ago?

EXERCISE

Invitation to Practice Awareness of Vicissitudes for Your Child

---

1. Calm and center the body.
2. What is painful or challenging in your child's life right now? Are they struggling with anything?
3. How is your relationship with them right now? Has it always been like this, or has it changed?
4. What is going well for your child? Are they healthy or mastering a life skill? Has this skill or blessing always been there, or has it changed?
5. What has resolved in your relationship with them? Do you understand more about them? Has this understanding always been here, or has it changed?

Expansion

Calm and settle the body with breath or finding stillness in yourself. Take a moment to ask yourself these questions. You may like to read them aloud and leave a space to reflect.

Is there gain in your life right now? Do you have enough money, enough food, and enough sleep? Is your life spacious, free, and full of comfort? When has there been abundance in your life before? Did it stay consistent, or did it change?

Is this a time of loss? Is there scarcity and lack—not enough money, not enough time, or maybe someone you love has left or died? When have you had loss before? Does the memory feel the same, or has it shifted with time to become more or less painful?

Do people think you are a great parent, a wonderful employee, a trustworthy and honest friend, or are there those who think you are pushy and overly concerned with your child, manipulative and irrational?

Right now, do folks love what you are doing? Are they happy with you and how skillful you are? Do you do good things in the world, get approval, and feel that you matter? Or are you disparaged, corrected, belittled, and told you don't know what you are doing or that you don't have good judgment?

Right now, are you in a beautiful place with pleasant sights, sounds, and smells, good food, company you like, and those who think and act in ways you approve of and share your idea of the world?

Is there physical pain in the body at this moment? Mental pain? Is there anxiety, guilt, uncertainty, confusion, or a feeling that somehow something is wrong? Are you surrounded by those you feel estranged and separate from? Is your heart contracted with the suffering of another or the shared pain in the world?

Rest in the awareness that you have already lived through great challenges and joys; you have experience with both of these. All of us have survived loss, pain, and suffering. We've all known joy and ease. Rest in this understanding, and trust our ability to do hard things. We've done hard things before, and we are still here.

Refection questions: What did you learn about yourself and your situation from considering these conditions?

EXERCISE

Invitation to Practice Just Listening Body Scan

Find a comfortable, supported posture, lying down if you choose. Begin by asking yourself if you would enjoy having your eyes open or closed and giving that to yourself. Rest comfortably, knowing the earth is supporting your body.

1. Calm and center yourself. Focus on returning to your breath if that is supportive. You can close your eyes or allow them to rest

on something you find soothing, like a beautiful color or something from nature.

2. Notice what is in your heart.
3. Ask, *What are you longing for?* Listen to your heart's answer.
4. What is the best gift you can offer this tender, feeling heart right now? How can you make life more beautiful for your heart?
5. Repeat the inquiry by asking your mind and body what they are longing for.

Expansion

Begin by sensing into the toes and feet, noticing what there is to notice. Feel the contact with fabric and floor; notice heat or cold. Ask your feet, *How are you, my feet?* Take time to listen. Don't rush to classify sensations or assign meaning; let the answer come from the body. When you understand how the feet are, ask, *What are you longing for?* It might be warmth or touch. When you know what this part of the body would enjoy, ask, *What is the best gift I can offer you?* Maybe it's a foot bath or a massage. Maybe it's rest. Continue this inquiry with your legs, back, belly, heart, arms, head, face, feelings, and mind, asking: *What do I need myself to know? What would make my life more beautiful?* Listen to the answer. This meditation can be as detailed as you would like, or you can streamline the inquiry to include three things: the body, the mind, and the heart.

When we understand the body, emotions, and mind, we have already begun creating the conditions of self-care. This body, mind, and heart are honest and authentic. The mind might long for beauty or something new—a different location or fresh experience that supports our joy of learning or delight in beauty. The mind and body may want rest—this doesn't mean we have to stop our lives or quit our jobs. It can simply mean we infuse responsive attunement into our day with the intention of care.

We can wash our hair gently with kindness or take time to wash our toes with a soapy washcloth in the shower, letting them know we are there for them. We can stop and sit down to enjoy a cup of tea in a café instead of taking it to go and drinking it in the car. If we long for beauty, a trip to a greenhouse to see bright begonias or tropical orchids in the winter can remind us that there are seasons of growth and light and seasons of slowness and recuperation. If we are longing for physical expression and joy, we can turn on our favorite song and dance in the kitchen (one of my favorite ways to nourish my joy). We can stop by a dog park and watch the dogs rolling on their backs, playing and chasing, and share in their happiness.

When we ask what we are longing for, this is not tanha, the thirst of craving the Buddha described as the source of suffering. Inquiring and listening bring us into relational self-compassion, not obsessive greed or self-centeredness. When we understand we are part of the healing process for our children and recognize that our happiness contributes to their happiness, we see that self-care and nourishing our joy are acts of caring for the world. Joy is part of our birthright, part of living in a body.

Meditation on Sky

In times when we are confronted with things that feel too big for us, and our ability to be a compassionate presence feels small, it is helpful to remember we are part of a much bigger cosmos, more connected than we may remember. You do not have to be in a specific posture for this meditation. It can be done in a hospital emergency room or in your backyard. Wherever you find yourself, look at the sky through a window or, better yet, stand outside. See the vastness of the sky. Watch the clouds, the shifting light or darkness, and any evidence of wind. Rest in this boundaryless part of the world. The sky is vast and holds all things: the sun, the moon, the earth, our solar system, me, and my child.

EXERCISE

Invitation to Practice Meditation on Sky

1. Look at the sky, preferably outdoors or through a window.
2. Breathing, feel the sky moving into your body. You can ask, "When does the sky become my breath, and when does my breath become the sky?"
3. Recognize the timeless and unstainable quality of the air.
4. See your own clarity, goodness, and vastness mirrored by the sky.
5. Rest in the purity of the sky, knowing our breath and body return to the sky.

Expansion

The sky is always there for us. The breath in this body is made of atoms as old as our planet. The oxygen I breathe in the atmosphere has been here for billions of years, before there was life on this planet, before my ancestors lived. It will be here after I am gone. This breath links me to the past and to the future. This breath, moving through me, makes my life possible. It is linked to the sky and has witnessed tornados, blizzards, and quiet sunrises. Nothing can mark this air I breathe. It reflects my own clarity, my own goodness, and my Buddha nature. I rest in this stainless purity of the air and the sky, knowing it is in me supporting my life and my child's. I am made of the sky. The sky is in this body, my breath, and the body of my child. The air in this body returns to the sky. The air in my child's body returns to the sky. It is all the same air.

Acknowledgments

I am grateful and honored by the parents who trusted me enough to share their stories and their pain. Your experiences are a gift to me and made writing this book possible. Thank you to the kids I work with, who touch my heart and demonstrate how healing is possible every day. Thank you to my husband, Rick, who has been my partner in life's adventures for over thirty years, for all the ways you show kindness, including feeding everyone while I was in grad school, lying on the couch writing and researching for two years. We would have starved without you. Thank you to Kate Pomeroy for helping to keep me somewhat sane and balanced through your patience and therapeutic skill. Thank you to Joe Houska, my empathy buddy, for making space in your life to show up for me and care, and a huge thank you to my Sangha, Earth Holders of Northwestern Connecticut, which gives me encouragement and gentleness. I'd like to acknowledge my children/teachers, Bella and James, who keep offering me the lessons I need to learn in this lifetime and help polish my rough edges in the most surprising ways. I'd never have learned these things without you.

And thank you to Parallax, to my editors Miranda Perrone and Jacob Surpin for your consistent encouragement and belief in the worth of this book. Thank you, Miranda, for letting me tell my story the way I needed to. Gratitude.

Notes

INTRODUCTION

1. National Institute of Mental Health, "Suicide," June 2022, www.nimh.nih.gov/health/statistics/suicide.

2. Resmaa Menakem, *My Grandmother's Hands: Racialized Trauma and the Pathway to Mending Our Hearts and Bodies* (Las Vegas, NV: Central Recovery Press, 2017).

3. David A. Treleaven, *Trauma-Sensitive Mindfulness: Practices for Safe and Transformative Healing.* (New York: W. W. Norton, 2018); Bissel A. van der Kolk, *The Body Keeps the Score: Brain, Mind, and Body in the Healing of Trauma* (New York: Viking, 2014).

4. Treleaven, *Trauma-Sensitive Mindfulness.*

I. THE PATH

1. Shelley E. Taylor, "Tend and Befriend Theory," in *Handbook of Theories of Social Psychology*, eds. Paul A.M. Van Lange, Arie W. Kruglanski, and E. Tory Higgins, 32–49 (Newberry Park, CA: Sage Publications, 2012), https://doi.org/10.4135/9781446249215.n3.

2. Taylor, "Tend and Befriend Theory."

3. Brad J. Bushman, "Does Venting Anger Feed or Extinguish the Flame? Catharsis, Rumination, Distraction, Anger, and Aggressive Responding," *Personality and Social Psychology Bulletin* 28:6 (2002), 724–31, https://doi.org/10.1177/0146167202289002; Thich Nhat Hanh, *Anger: Wisdom for Cooling the Flames* (New York: Penguin, 2002).

2. THE TRUTH OF SUFFERING

1. David B. Chamberlain, "Babies Remember Pain," *Pre- and Perinatal Psychology Journal* 3:4 (1989), 297–310; William R. Emerson, "Birth Trauma: The Psychological Effects of Obstetrical Interventions," *Journal of Prenatal & Perinatal Psychology & Health* 13:1 (1998), 11–44, https://doi.org/10.1007/978-3-030-41716-1_36.

2. Chamberlain, "Babies Remember Pain."

3. Gil Fronsdal, *The Issue at Hand: Essays on Buddhist Mindfulness Practice*, 2001, www.insightmeditationcenter.org/books-articles /the-issue-at-hand.

4. Francis Story, *The Three Basic Facts of Existence II: Suffering (Dukkha)* (Kandy, Sri Lanka: Buddhist Publication Society, 1973), www.bps.lk /olib/wh/wh191_Burton-etal_Three-Basic-Facts-of-Existance --II-Dukkha.pdf.

5. Insight Meditation Center, "Dhamma Lists," 2023, www.insightmeditationcenter.org/books-articles/dhamma-lists.

6. Thich Nhat Hanh, *The Heart of the Buddha's Teaching: Transforming Suffering into Peace, Joy, and Liberation* (New York: Broadway, 1998), 19; Kamala Masters, "Four Noble Truths, Day 2," Dharma Seed, January 24, 2015.

7. Masters, "Four Noble Truths, Day 2."

8. Pema Chödrön, *When Things Fall Apart: Heart Advice for Difficult Times* (Boston: Shambhala, 1997), 11.

9. Thich Nhat Hanh, *No Mud, No Lotus: The Art of Transforming Suffering* (Berkeley, CA: Parallax Press, 2014), 1.

10. Peter Dudley, "Pain Pathways," Teach Me Physiology, 2021, https: //teachmephysiology.com/nervous-system/sensory-system /pain-pathways.

11. Ranae J. Evenson and Robin W. Simon, "Clarifying the Relationship between Parenthood and Depression," *Journal of Health and Social Behavior* 46:4 (2005), 341–58, https:// doi.org/10.1177/002214650504600403.

12. Ṭhānissaro Bhikkhu, trans., "Maha-hatthipadopama Sutta: The Great Elephant Footprint Simile (MN 28)," Access to Insight (BCBS Edition), 2013, www.accesstoinsight.org/tipitaka /mn/mn.028.than.html.

13. Masters, "Four Noble Truths, Day 2."

14. Thich Nhat Hanh, *Heart of the Buddha's Teaching*, 44.

15. Bhikkhu Bodhi, *The Noble Eightfold Path: Way to the End of Suffering* (Kandy, Sri Lanka: Buddhist Publication Society, 1998), 8.

16. Bodhi, *Noble Eightfold Path*, 10.

17. Thich Nhat Hanh, *Heart of the Buddha's Teaching*, 43.

18. Thich Nhat Hanh, *Heart of the Buddha's Teaching*, 123–24.

3. NOT ABANDONING

1. Akincano Marc Weber, "Setting to Sea in the Leaky Boat of Self (Upadana)," Dharma Seed, July 14, 2014.

2. Maurice O'Connell Walshe, trans., "Attadiipaa Sutta: An Island to Oneself (SN 22.43)," Access to Insight (BCBS Edition), 2013, www.accesstoinsight.org/tipitaka/sn/sn22/sn22.043.wlsh.html.

3. Akincano Marc Weber, "Hedonic Hotspots, Hedonic Potholes: Vedanā Revisited," *Contemporary Buddhism* 19:1 (2018), 7–30.

4. Joseph Goldstein, *Mindfulness: A Practical Guide to Awakening* (Louisville, CO: Sounds True, 2010), 57.

5. Gaëlle Desbordes, Tim Gard, Elizabeth A. Hoge, Britta K. Hölzel, Catherine Kerr, Sara W. Lazar, Andrew Olendzki, and David R. Vago, "Moving beyond Mindfulness: Defining Equanimity as an Outcome Measure in Meditation and Contemplative Research," *Mindfulness* 6:2 (April 2015), 356–72, https://doi.org/10.1007/s12671-013-0269-8.

6. Desbordes et al., "Moving beyond Mindfulness"; Christina Feldman, *Boundless Heart: The Buddhist Path of Kindness, Compassion, Joy, and Equanimity* (Boulder, CO: Shambhala, 2017); Donald Rothberg, *The Engaged Spiritual Life: A Buddhist Approach to Transforming Ourselves* (Boston: Beacon, 2006).

7. Dalai Lama, *An Open Heart: Practicing Compassion in Everyday Life* (New York: Little, Brown, 2001), 162.

8. Dalai Lama, *An Open Heart*; Desbordes et al., "Moving beyond Mindfulness."

9. Akincano Marc Weber, "Brahmavihārās: At the Heart of Human Experience," Dharma Seed, July 7, 2015.

10. Nyanaponika Thera, trans., "Sallatha Sutta: The Dart (SN 36.6)," Access to Insight (BCBS Edition), 2010, www.accesstoinsight.org/tipitaka/sn/sn36/sn36.006.nypo.html.

4. THE EIGHT WORLDLY WINDS

1. Rothberg, *The Engaged Spiritual Life.*

2. Centers for Disease Control and Prevention (CDC), "Leading Indicators for Chronic Diseases and Risk Factors," 2022, https://chronicdata.cdc.gov.

3. Sister Vajira and Francis Story, trans., "Maha-parinibbana Sutta: Last Days of the Buddha (DN 16)," Access to Insight (BCBS Edition), 2013, www.accesstoinsight.org/tipitaka/dn/dn.16.1-6.vaji.html.

4. Tara Brach, "The Power of the Pause," *Spirituality + Health,* August 2003, www.spiritualityhealth.com/articles/2012/01/28/power-pause.

5. Ajahn Sumedho, *Ajahn Sumedho: The Anthology, vol. 3: Direct Realization* (Hempstead, UK: Amaravati, 2014), 239.

5. MEDITATION TO NOURISH OUR STABILITY

1. Desbordes et al., "Moving beyond Mindfulness."

2. Brother Phap Hai, *Nothing to It: Ten Ways to Be at Home with Yourself* (Berkeley, CA: Parallax Press, 2015).

3. Britta K. Hölzel, James Carmody, Mark Vangel, Christina Congleton, Sita M. Yerramsetti, Tim Gard, and Sara W. Lazar, "Mindfulness Practice Leads to Increases in Regional Brain Gray Matter Density," *Psychiatry Research* 191:1 (2011), 36–43, https://doi.org/10.1016/j.pscychresns.2010.08.006.

4. Desbordes et al., "Moving beyond Mindfulness."

5. Alvin Powell, "When Science Meets Mindfulness," *Harvard Gazette,* April 9, 2018, https://news.harvard.edu/gazette/story/2018/04/harvard-researchers-study-how-mindfulness-may-change-the-brain-in-depressed-patients/.

6. Desbordes et al., "Moving beyond Mindfulness," 7.

7. Ṭhānissaro Bhikkhu, trans., "Maha-Rahulovada Sutta: The Greater Exhortation to Rahula (MN 62)," Access to Insight (BCBS Edition), 2013, www.accesstoinsight.org/tipitaka/mn/mn.062.than.html.

8. Ṭhānissaro Bhikkhu, "Maha-Rahulovada Sutta."

9. Ṭhānissaro Bhikkhu, "Maha-Rahulovada Sutta."

6. GRANDMA KNOWLEDGE

1. K. R. Sonneville and S. K. Lipson, "Disparities in Eating Disorder Diagnosis and Treatment According to Weight Status, Race /Ethnicity, Socioeconomic Background, and Sex among College Students," *International Journal of Eating Disorders* 51:6 (2018), 518–26, https://doi.org/10.1002/eat.22846.

2. J. E. Pate, A. J. Pumariega, C. Hester, and D. M. Garner, "Cross-cultural Patterns in Eating Disorders: A Review," *Journal of the American Academy of Child & Adolescent Psychiatry* 31:5 (1992), 802–09.

3. Jan Chozen Bays, *Mindful Eating: A Guide to Rediscovering a Healthy and Joyful Relationship with Food* (Boston: HarperCollins, 2009).

4. Bays, *Mindful Eating*.

5. Consensus Conference Panel, "Recommended Amount of Sleep for a Healthy Adult: A Joint Consensus Statement of the American Academy of Sleep Medicine and Sleep Research Society," *Sleep* 38:6 (2015), 843–44, https://doi.org/10.5665/sleep.4716.

6. Allison G. Harvey, Greg Murray, Rebecca A. Chandler, and Adriane Soehner, "Sleep Disturbance as Transdiagnostic: Consideration of Neurobiological Mechanisms," *Clinical Psychology Review* 31:2 (2011), 225–35, https://doi.org/10.1016/j.cpr.2010.04.003.

7. John W. Schroeder, *Skillful Means: The Heart of Buddhist Compassion* (Honolulu: University of Hawaii Press, 2001).

8. Ṭhānissaro Bhikkhu, trans., "Sona Sutta: About Sona (AN 6.55)," Access to Insight (BCBS Edition), 2013, www.accesstoinsight.org/tipitaka/an/an02/an02.031.than.html.

9. Nicola Petrocchi and Alessandro Couyoumdjian, "The Impact of Gratitude on Depression and Anxiety: The Mediating Role of Criticizing, Attacking, and Reassuring the Self," *Self and Identity* 15:2 (2016), 191–205, https://doi.org/10.1080/15298868.2015.1095794.

10. Stephen M. Yoshimura and Kassandra Berzins, "Grateful Experiences and Expressions: The Role of Gratitude Expressions in the Link between Gratitude Experiences and Well-being," *Review of Communication* 17:2 (2017), 106–18, https://doi.org/10.1080/15358593.2017.1293836.

7. EMPATHY AND COMPASSION

1. Daniel J. Siegel, *Mindsight: The New Science of Personal Transformation* (New York: Bantam, 2010), 167.

2. Tania Singer, Ben Seymour, John O'Doherty, Holger Kaube, Raymond J. Dolan, and Chris D. Frith, "Empathy for Pain Involves the Affective but Not Sensory Components of Pain," *Science* 303:20 (2004), 1157–62, https://doi.org/10.1126/science.1093535.

3. Tania Singer and Olga M. Klimecki, "Empathy and Compassion," *Current Biology* 24:18 (2014), 875, https://doi.org/10.1016/j.cub.2014.06.054.

4. Paul Gilbert, *Depression: The Evolution of Powerlessness* (London: Routledge, 1992); Matthis Synofzik, Gottfried Vosgerau, and Martin Voss, "The Experience of Agency: An Interplay between Prediction and Postdiction," *Frontiers in Psychology* 4:127 (2013), 1–8, https://doi.org/10.3389/ fpsyg.2013.00127; Paul Wilner and Richard C. Goldstein, "Mediation of Depression by Perceptions of Defeat and Entrapment in High-Stress Mothers," *British Journal of Medical Psychology* 74:4 (2001), 473–85, https://doi.org/10.1348/000711201161127.

5. Lyn Y. Abramson, Martin E. Seligman, and John D. Teasdale, "Learned Helplessness in Humans: Critique and Reformulation," *Journal of Abnormal Psychology* 87:1 (1978), 49–74, https://doi.org/10.1037/0021-843X.87.1.49.

6. Laura E. Simons, Liesbet Goubert, Tine Vervoort, and David Borsook, "Circles of Engagement: Childhood Pain and Parent Brain," *Neuroscience Biobehavioral Review* 68 (2016), 540, https://doi.org/10.1016/j.neubiorev.2016.06.020.

7. Akincano Marc Weber, "Brahmavihārās, as Practices for the Relational World," Dharma Seed, July 3, 2017.

8. Singer and Klimecki, "Empathy and Compassion."

9. Singer et al., "Empathy for Pain," 1559.

10. Gilbert, *Depression*; Wilner and Goldstein, "Mediation of Depression."

11. Nancy Eisenberg, Carlos Valiente, Amanda Sheffield Morris, Richard A. Fabes, Amanda Cumberland, Mark Reiser, Elizabeth Thompson Gershoff, et al., "Longitudinal Relations among Parental Emotional Expressivity, Children's Regulation, and Quality of Socioemotional Functioning," *Developmental Psychology* 39:1 (2003), 3–19, https://doi.org/10.1037//0012-1649.39.1.3; Richard A. Fabes, Stacie A. Leonard, Kristina Kupanoff, and Carol Lynn Martin, "Parental Coping with Children's Negative Emotions: Relations with Children's Emotional and Social Responding," *Child Development* 72:3 (2001), 907–20, https://doi.org/10.1111/1467-8624.00323; Jennifer L. Hudson, Jonathan S. Comer, and Philip C. Kendall, "Parental Responses to Positive and Negative Emotions in Anxious and Nonanxious Children," *Journal of ClinicalChild and Adolescent Psychology* 37:2 (2008), 303–13, https://doi.org/10.1080 /15374410801955839; Simons et al., "Circles of Engagement"; Singer and Klimecki, "Empathy and Compassion"; H. A. van Oers, L. Haverman, P. F. Limperg, E. M. van Dijk-Lokkart, H. Maurice-Stam, and M. A. Grootenhuis, "Anxiety and Depression in Mothers and Fathers of a Chronically Ill Child," *Maternal and Child Health Journal* 18:8 (2014), https://doi.org/10.1007/s10995-014-1445-8.

12. Eisenberg et al., "Longitudinal Relations"; Fabes et al., "Parental Coping"; Hudson et al., "Parental Responses"; Simons et al., "Circles of Engagement"; Singer and Klimecki, "Empathy and Compassion"; van Oers et al., "Anxiety and Depression."

13. Feldman, *Boundless Heart.*

14. Weber, "Brahmavihārās, as Practices for the Relational World."

15. Weber, "Brahmavihārās, as Practices for the Relational World."

16. Weber, "Brahmavihārās, as Practices for the Relational World."

17. Ṭhānissaro Bhikkhu, trans., "Mettā (Mettānisamsa) Sutta: Good Will (AN 11.16)," Access to Insight (BCBS Edition), 2013, www.accesstoinsight.org/tipitaka/an/an11/an11.016.than.html.

18. Weber, "Brahmavihārās, as Practices for the Relational World."

19. Feldman, *Boundless Heart.*

20. Shelly Graf, "Sharon Salzberg on Mettā: The Song of the Heart," Common Ground Meditation Center, October 10, 2013, https:// commongroundmeditation.org/all/reflection/sharon-salzberg -on-metta-the-song-of-the-heart.

8. KARMA AND INTENTION

1. Andrew Olendzki, *Unlimiting Mind: The Radical Experimental Psychology of Buddhism* (Somerville, MA: Wisdom, 2010), 145.

2. Thich Nhat Hanh, *Understanding Our Mind: 50 Verses on Buddhist Psychology* (Berkeley, CA: Parallax Press, 2006), 44.

3. Olendzki, *Unlimiting Mind*, 29.

4. Rothberg, *The Engaged Spiritual Life*, 60.

5. Singer et al., "Empathy for Pain."

6. Thich Nhat Hanh, *Heart of the Buddha's Teaching*, 124.

7. Feldman, *Boundless Heart*, 64.

9. THE PEACE OF EQUANIMITY

1. Kamala Masters, "Understanding Equanimity, Day 3," Dharma Seed, January 25, 2015.

2. Anālayo, *Compassion and Emptiness in Early Buddhism* (Cambridge, UK: Windhorse, 2015); Feldman, *Boundless Heart*; Kamala Masters, "1st Day of Equanimity Instructions: Developing Equanimity for Neutral Person and Benefactor," Dharma Seed, May 16, 2018; Masters, "Understanding Equanimity, Day 3"; Rothberg, *The Engaged Spiritual Life*.

3. Desbordes et al., "Moving beyond Mindfulness"; Olendzki, *Unlimiting Mind*.

4. Nyanaponika Thera, trans., "The Four Sublime States: Contemplations on Love, Compassion, Sympathetic Joy and Equanimity," Access to Insight (BCBS Edition), 2013, www.accesstoinsight.org /lib/authors/nyanaponika/wheel006.html.

5. Desbordes et al., "Moving beyond Mindfulness," 358; Thich Nhat Hanh, *Heart of the Buddha's Teaching*.

6. Gil Fronsdal, "Equanimity," Insight Meditation Society, 2004, www.insightmeditationcenter.org/books-articles/equanimity.

7. Thich Nhat Hanh, *Heart of the Buddha's Teaching*, 161.

8. Anālayo, *Compassion and Emptiness*; Desbordes et al., "Moving beyond Mindfulness"; Feldman, *Boundless Heart*; Rothberg, *The Engaged Spiritual Life*.

9. Bhikkhu Sujato, trans., "At Sedaka: A Plain Translation of the Saṁyutta Nikāya (SN 47.19)," *Linked Discourses on Mindfulness Meditation*, Sutta Central, 2018, https://suttacentral.net/sn47.19 /en/sujato.

10. Masters, "Understanding Equanimity, Day 3."

11. Masters, "Understanding Equanimity, Day 3."

12. Desbordes et al., "Moving beyond Mindfulness," 361.

13. Anālayo, *Compassion and Emptiness*; Rothberg, *The Engaged Spiritual Life*.

14. Masters, "Understanding Equanimity, Day 3"; Masters, "1st Day of Equanimity Instructions."

15. Masters, "1st Day of Equanimity Instructions."

16. Desbordes et al., "Moving beyond Mindfulness," 9; Masters, "Understanding Equanimity, Day 3"; Masters, "1st Day of Equanimity Instructions."

17. Desbordes et al., "Moving beyond Mindfulness"; Thich Nhat Hanh, *Heart of the Buddha's Teaching*; Masters, "Understanding Equanimity, Day 3"; Masters, "1st Day of Equanimity Instructions."

18. Masters, "1st Day of Equanimity Instructions."

19. Desbordes et al., "Moving beyond Mindfulness"; Jon Kabat-Zinn and Myla Kabat-Zinn, *The Healing Power of Mindful Parenting*, video, Psychotherapy.net, 2012, www.psychotherapy.net/video/kabat-zinn -mindful-parenting; Masters, "1st Day of Equanimity Instructions."

20. Desbordes et al., "Moving beyond Mindfulness," 13.

21. Desbordes et al., "Moving beyond Mindfulness," 365.

22. Desbordes et al., "Moving beyond Mindfulness," 12.

23. Hudson et al., "Parental Responses."

24. Simons et al., "Circles of Engagement," 543.

25. Simons et al., "Circles of Engagement."

26. Sasha G. Aschenbrand and Philip C. Kendall, "The Effect of Perceived Child Anxiety Status on Parental Latency to Intervene with Anxious and Nonanxious Youth," *Journal of Consulting and Clinical Psychology* 80:2 (2012), 232–38, https://doi.org/10.1037/a0027230; Hudson et al., "Parental Responses"; Chris Segrin, Michelle Givertz, Paulina Swaitkowski, and Neil Montgomery, "Overparenting Is Associated with Child Problems and a Critical Family Environment," *Journal of Child and Family Studies* 24:2 (2015), 470–79, https://doi.org/10.1007/s10826-013-9858-3.; Simons et al., "Circles of Engagement."

27. Aschenbrand and Kendall, "Effect of Perceived Child Anxiety Status"; Hudson et al., "Parental Responses."

28. Desbordes et al., "Moving beyond Mindfulness"; Gil Fronsdal and Sayadaw U Pandita, "A Perfect Balance: Cultivating Equanimity with Gil Fronsdal and Sayadaw U Pandita," *Tricycle,* Winter 2005, https://tricycle.org/magazine/cultivate-equanimity.

10. RIDING THE WAVES

1. Akincano Marc Weber, "Brahmavihārās: At the Heart of Human Experience," Dharma Seed, July 7, 2015.

2. Mark Nunberg, "Compassion and Equanimity Practice," Dharma Seed, March 10, 2019.

3. Nunberg, "Compassion and Equanimity Practice."

4. Pema Chödrön, *Tonglen: The Path of Transformation* (Halifax, Canada: Kalapa, 2001).

5. Chödrön, *Tonglen*, 10.

CODA

1. Thich Nhat Hanh, *Two Treasures: Buddhist Teachings on Awakening and True Happiness* (Berkeley, CA: Parallax Press, 2003).

Bibliography

Abramson, Lyn Y., Martin E. Seligman, and John D. Teasdale. "Learned Helplessness in Humans: Critique and Reformulation." *Journal of Abnormal Psychology* 87:1 (1978), 49–74. https://doi.org/10.1037/0021-843X.87.1.49.

Anālayo. *Compassion and Emptiness in Early Buddhism.* Cambridge, UK: Windhorse, 2015.

Anālayo. *Satipatthāna: The Direct Path to Realization.* Cambridge, UK: Windhorse, 2003.

Aschenbrand, Sasha G., and Philip C. Kendall. "The Effect of Perceived Child Anxiety Status on Parental Latency to Intervene with Anxious and Nonanxious Youth." *Journal of Consulting and Clinical Psychology* 80:2 (2012), 232–38. https://doi.org/10.1037/a0027230.

Bays, Jan Chozen. *Mindful Eating: A Guide to Rediscovering a Healthy and Joyful Relationship with Food.* Boston: HarperCollins, 2009.

Bhadantácariya Buddhaghosa. *The path of purification (Visuddhimagga).* Translated by Bhikkhu Ñāṇamoli. Kandy, Sri Lanka: Buddhist Publication Society, 2010. www.accesstoinsight.org/lib/authors/nanamoli/PathofPurification2011.pdf.

Bodhi, Bhikkhu. *The Noble Eightfold Path: Way to the End of Suffering.* Kandy, Sri Lanka: Buddhist Publication Society, 1998.

Bodhipaksa. "We Are What We Think." *Tricycle,* Fall 2014.

Boorstein, Sylvia. *Pay Attention, for Goodness' Sake: Practicing the Perfections of the Heart; the Buddhist Path of Kindness.* New York: Ballentine, 2002.

Brach, Tara. "The Power of the Pause." *Spirituality + Health,* August 2003. www.spiritualityhealth.com/articles/2012/01/28/power-pause.

Bushman, Brad J. "Does Venting Anger Feed or Extinguish the Flame? Catharsis, Rumination, Distraction, Anger, and Aggressive Responding." *Personality and Social Psychology Bulletin* 28:6 (2002), 724–31. https://doi.org/10.1177/0146167202289002.

Centers for Disease Control and Prevention (CDC). "Leading Indicators for Chronic Diseases and Risk Factors." 2022. https://chronicdata.cdc.gov.

Chamberlain, David B. "Babies Remember Pain." *Pre- and Perinatal Psychology Journal* 3:4 (1989), 297–310.

Chödrön, Pema. *Tonglen: The Path of Transformation.* Halifax, Canada: Kalapa, 2001.

Chödrön, Pema. *When Things Fall Apart: Heart Advice for Difficult Times.* Boston: Shambhala, 1997.

Consensus Conference Panel. "Recommended Amount of Sleep for a Healthy Adult: A Joint Consensus Statement of the American Academy of Sleep Medicine and Sleep Research Society." *Sleep* 38:6 (2015), 843–44. https://doi.org/10.5665/sleep.4716.

Conze, Edward, translator. *The Large Sutra on Perfect Wisdom with the Divisions of the Abhisamayalankara.* Berkeley, CA: University of California Press, 1997.

Dalai Lama. *An Open Heart: Practicing Compassion in Everyday Life.* New York: Little, Brown, 2001.

Dass, Ram, and Stephen Levine. *Grist for the Mill: Awakening to Oneness.* New York: HarperOne, 2014.

Desbordes, Gaëlle, Tim Gard, Elizabeth A. Hoge, Britta K. Hölzel, Catherine Kerr, Sara W. Lazar, Andrew Olendzki, and David R. Vago. "Moving beyond Mindfulness: Defining Equanimity as an Outcome Measure in Meditation and Contemplative Research." *Mindfulness* 6:2 (April 2015), 356–72. https://doi.org/10.1007/s12671-013-0269-8.

Dudley, Peter. "Pain Pathways." Teach Me Physiology. 2021. https://teachmephysiology.com/nervous-system/sensory-system/pain-pathways.

Eisenberg, Nancy, Carlos Valiente, Amanda Sheffield Morris, Richard A. Fabes, Amanda Cumberland, Mark Reiser, Elizabeth Thompson Gershoff, Stephanie A Shepard, and Sandra Losoya. "Longitudinal Relations among Parental Emotional Expressivity, Children's Regulation, and Quality of Socioemotional Functioning." *Developmental Psychology* 39:1 (2003), 3–19. https://doi.org/10.1037//0012-1649.39.1.3.

Emerson, William R. "Birth Trauma: The Psychological Effects of Obstetrical Interventions." *Journal of Prenatal & Perinatal Psychology & Health* 13:1 (1998), 11–44. https://doi.org/10.1007/978-3-030-41716-1_36.

Epstein, Mark. *Thoughts Without a Thinker: Psychotherapy from a Buddhist Perspective.* New York: Basic Books, 1995.

Evenson, Ranae J., and Robin W. Simon. "Clarifying the Relationship between Parenthood and Depression." *Journal of Health and Social Behavior* 46:4 (2005), 341–58. https://doi.org/10.1177/002214650504600403.

Fabes, Richard A., Stacie A. Leonard, Kristina Kupanoff, and Carol Lynn Martin. "Parental Coping with Children's Negative Emotions: Relations with Children's Emotional and Social Responding." *Child Development* 72:3 (2001), 907–20. https://doi.org/10.1111/1467-8624.00323.

Feldman, Christina. *Boundless Heart: The Buddhist Path of Kindness, Compassion, Joy, and Equanimity.* Boulder, CO: Shambhala, 2017.

Fronsdal, Gil. "Equanimity." Insight Meditation Society. 2004. www.insightmeditationcenter.org/books-articles/equanimity.

Fronsdal, Gil. *The Issue at Hand: Essays on Buddhist Mindfulness Practice.* 2001. www.insightmeditationcenter.org/books-articles/the-issue-at-hand.

Fronsdal, Gil, and Sayadaw U Pandita. "A Perfect Balance: Cultivating Equanimity with Gil Fronsdal and Sayadaw U Pandita." *Tricycle,* Winter 2005. https://tricycle.org/magazine/cultivate-equanimity.

Gilbert, Paul. *Depression: The Evolution of Powerlessness.* London: Routledge, 1992.

Goldstein, Joseph. *Mindfulness: A Practical Guide to Awakening.* Louisville, CO: Sounds True, 2010.

Goleman, Daniel. "Hot to Help: When Can Empathy Move Us to Action?" *Greater Good Magazine,* March 1, 2008. https://greatergood.berkeley.edu/article/item/hot_to_help.

Graf, Shelly. "Sharon Salzberg on Mettā: The Song of the Heart." Common Ground Meditation Center. October 10, 2013. https://commongroundmeditation.org/all/reflection/sharon-salzberg-on-metta-the-song-of-the-heart.

Hai, Brother Phap. *Nothing to It: Ten Ways to Be at Home with Yourself.* Berkeley, CA: Parallax Press, 2015.

Harvey, Allison G., Greg Murray, Rebecca A. Chandler, and Adriane Soehner. "Sleep Disturbance as Transdiagnostic: Consideration of Neurobiological Mechanisms." *Clinical Psychology Review* 31:2 (2011), 225–35. https://doi.org/10.1016/j.cpr.2010.04.003.

Hirshfield, Jane. *Women in Praise of the Sacred: 43 Centuries of Spiritual Poetry by Women.* New York: Harper Perennial, 1995.

Hölzel, Britta K., James Carmody, Mark Vangel, Christina Congleton, Sita M. Yerramsetti, Tim Gard, and Sara W. Lazar. "Mindfulness Practice Leads to Increases in Regional Brain Gray Matter Density." *Psychiatry Research* 191:1 (2011), 36–43. https://doi.org/10.1016/j.pscychresns.2010.08.006.

Hudson, Jennifer L., Jonathan S. Comer, and Philip C. Kendall. "Parental Responses to Positive and Negative Emotions in Anxious and Nonanxious Children." *Journal of Clinical Child and Adolescent Psychology* 37:2 (2008), 303–13. https://doi.org/10.1080/15374410801955839.

Insight Meditation Center. "Dhamma Lists." 2023. www.insightmeditationcenter.org/books-articles/dhamma-lists.

Kabat-Zinn, Jon, and Myla Kabat-Zinn. *The Healing Power of Mindful Parenting.* Video. Psychotherapy.net. 2012. www.psychotherapy.net/video/kabat-zinn-mindful-parenting.

Klimecki, Olga M., Susanne Leiberg, Claus Lamm, and Tania Singer. "Functional Neural Plasticity and Associated Changes in Positive Affect after Compassion Training." *Cerebral Cortex* 23:7 (2012), 1552–61. https://doi.org/10.1093/cercor/bhs142.

Klimecki, Olga M., Susanne Leiberg, Matthieu Ricard, and Tania Singer. "Differential Pattern of Functional Brain Plasticity after Compassion and Empathy Training." *Social Cognitive and Affective Neuroscience* 9:6 (2013), 873–79. https://doi.org/10.1093/scan/nst060.

Kornfield, Jack. "Meditation on Equanimity." On Jack Kornfield's official website. 2019. https://jackkornfield.com/meditation-equanimity.

Lazar, Sara W., Catherine E. Kerr, Rachel H. Wasserman, Jeremy R. Gray, Douglas N. Greve, Michael T. Treadway, Metta McGarvey, Brian T. Quinn, Jeffery A. Dusek, Herbert Benson, et al. "Meditation Experience Is Associated with Increased Cortical Thickness." *Neuroreport* 16:17 (2005), 1893–97. https://doi.org/10.1097/01.wnr.0000186598.66243.19.

Maitreya, Ananda, translator. *The Dhammapada.* Berkeley, CA: Parallax Press, 1995.

Masters, Kamala. "1st Day of Equanimity Instructions: Developing Equanimity for Neutral Person and Benefactor." Dharma Seed, May 16, 2018.

Masters, Kamala. "Four Noble Truths, Day 2." Dharma Seed, January 24, 2015a.

Masters, Kamala. "Understanding Equanimity, Day 3." Dharma Seed, January 25, 2015b.

Menakem, Resmaa. *My Grandmother's Hands: Racialized Trauma and the Pathway to Mending Our Hearts and Bodies.* Las Vegas, NV: Central Recovery Press, 2017.

Ñāṇamoli, Bhikkhu, and Bhikkhu Bodhi, translator. "Sallekha Sutta (MN 8.16)." *The Middle Length Discourses of the Buddha,* 4th ed. Somerville, MA: Wisdom, 1995.

National Institute of Mental Health. "Suicide." June 2022. www.nimh.nih .gov/health/statistics/suicide.

Nhat Hanh, Thich. *Anger: Wisdom for Cooling the Flames.* New York: Penguin, 2002.

Nhat Hanh, Thich. *Answers from the Heart: Practical Responses to Life's Burning Questions.* Berkeley, CA: Parallax Press, 2009.

Nhat Hanh, Thich. *The Art of Living: Peace and Freedom in the Here and Now.* New York: HarperOne, 2017.

Nhat Hanh, Thich. *Going Home: Jesus and Buddha as Brothers.* Berkeley, CA: Parallax Press, 2005.

Nhat Hanh, Thich. *The Heart of the Buddha's Teaching: Transforming Suffering into Peace, Joy, and Liberation.* New York: Broadway, 1998.

Nhat Hanh, Thich. *No Mud, No Lotus: The Art of Transforming Suffering.* Berkeley, CA: Parallax Press, 2014.

Nhat Hanh, Thich. "Thich Nhat Hanh Dharma Talks: Mettā Meditation." TNHAudio.org. 2010. https://tnhaudio.org/tag/metta-meditation.

Nhat Hanh, Thich. *Two Treasures: Buddhist Teachings on Awakening and True Happiness.* Berkeley, CA: Parallax Press, 2003.

Nhat Hanh, Thich. *Understanding Our Mind: 50 Verses on Buddhist Psychology.* Berkeley, CA: Parallax Press, 2006.

Nunberg, Mark. "Compassion and Equanimity Practice." Dharma Seed, March 10, 2019.

Olendzki, Andrew. *Unlimiting Mind: The Radical Experimental Psychology of Buddhism.* Somerville, MA: Wisdom, 2010.

Pate, J. E., A. J. Pumariega, C. Hester, and D. M. Garner. "Cross-cultural Patterns in Eating Disorders: A Review." *Journal of the American Academy of Child & Adolescent Psychiatry* 31:5 (1992), 802–09.

Petrocchi, Nicola, and Alessandro Couyoumdjian. "The Impact of Gratitude on Depression and Anxiety: The Mediating Role of Criticizing, Attacking, and Reassuring the Self." *Self and Identity* 15:2 (2016), 191–205. https://doi.org/10.1080/15298868.2015.1095794.

Powell, Alvin. "When Science Meets Mindfulness." *Harvard Gazette,* April 9, 2018. https://news.harvard.edu/gazette/story/2018/04/harvard -researchers-study-how-mindfulness-may-change-the-brain-in -depressed-patients/.

Rogers, Carl R. "Empathic: An Unappreciated Way of Being." *Counseling Psychologist* 5:2 (1975), 2–10. https://doi .org/10.1177/001100007500500202.

Rothberg, Donald. *The Engaged Spiritual Life: A Buddhist Approach to Transforming Ourselves.* Boston: Beacon, 2006.

Schroeder, John W. *Skillful Means: The Heart of Buddhist Compassion.* Honolulu: University of Hawaii Press, 2001.

Segrin, Chris, Michelle Givertz, Paulina Swaitkowski, and Neil Montgomery. "Overparenting Is Associated with Child Problems and a Critical Family Environment." *Journal of Child and Family Studies* 24:2 (2015), 470–79. https://doi.org/10.1007/s10826-013-9858-3.

Siegel, Daniel J. *Mindsight: The New Science of Personal Transformation.* New York: Bantam, 2010.

Simons, Laura E., Liesbet Goubert, Tine Vervoort, and David Borsook. "Circles of Engagement: Childhood Pain and Parent Brain." *Neuroscience Biobehavioral Review* 68 (2016), 537–46. https: //doi.org/10.1016/j.neubiorev.2016.06.020.

Singer, Tania, and Olga M. Klimecki. "Empathy and Compassion." *Current Biology* 24:18 (2014), 875–78. https://doi.org/10.1016 /j.cub.2014.06.054.

Singer, Tania, Ben Seymour, John O'Doherty, Holger Kaube, Raymond J. Dolan, and Chris D. Frith. "Empathy for Pain Involves the Affective but Not Sensory Components of Pain." *Science* 303:20 (2004), 1157–62. https://doi.org/10.1126/science.1093535.

Sonneville, K. R., and S. K. Lipson. "Disparities in Eating Disorder Diagnosis and Treatment According to Weight Status, Race/Ethnicity, Socioeconomic Background, and Sex among College Students." *International Journal of Eating Disorders* 51:6 (2018), 518–26. https: //doi.org/10.1002/eat.22846.

Story, Francis. *The Three Basic Facts of Existence II: Suffering (Dukkha).* Kandy, Sri Lanka: Buddhist Publication Society, 1973. www.bps.lk /olib/wh/wh191_Burton-etal_Three-Basic-Facts-of-Existance--II -Dukkha.pdf.

Sujato, Bhikkhu, translator. "At Sedaka: A Plain Translation of the Saṁyutta Nikāya (SN 47.19)." *Linked Discourses on Mindfulness Meditation.* Sutta Central. 2018. https://suttacentral.net/sn47.19/en/sujato.

Sumedho, Ajahn. *Ajahn Sumedho: The Anthology, vol. 3: Direct Realization.* Hempstead, UK: Amaravati, 2014.

Synofzik, Matthis, Gottfried Vosgerau, and Martin Voss. "The Experience of Agency: An Interplay between Prediction and Postdiction." *Frontiers in Psychology* 4:127 (2013), 1–8. https://doi.org/10.3389/fpsyg.2013.00127.

Taylor, Shelley E. "Tend and Befriend Theory." In Paul A. M. Van Lange, Arie W. Kruglanski, and E. Tory Higgins, eds., *Handbook of Theories of Social Psychology,* 32–49. Newberry Park, CA: Sage Publications, 2012. https://doi.org/10.4135/9781446249215.n3.

Ṭhānissaro Bhikkhu, translator. "Dhammacakkappavattana Sutta: Setting the Wheel of Dhamma in Motion (SN 56.11)." Access to Insight (BCBS Edition). 2013b. www.accesstoinsight.org/tipitaka/sn/sn56/sn56.011.than.html.

Ṭhānissaro Bhikkhu, translator. "Kataññu Suttas: Gratitude (AN 2.31–32)." Access to Insight (BCBS Edition). 2013c. www.accesstoinsight.org/tipitaka/an/an02/an02.031.than.html.

Ṭhānissaro Bhikkhu, translator. "Lokavipatti Sutta: The Failings of the World (AN 8.6)." Access to Insight (BCBS Edition). 2010. www.accesstoinsight.org/tipitaka/an/an08/an08.006.than.html.

Ṭhānissaro Bhikkhu, translator. "Maha-hatthipadopama Sutta: The Great Elephant Footprint Simile (MN 28)." Access to Insight (BCBS Edition). 2013d. www.accesstoinsight.org/tipitaka/mn/mn.028.than.html.

Ṭhānissaro Bhikkhu, translator. "Maha-Rahulovada Sutta: The Greater Exhortation to Rahula (MN 62)." Access to Insight (BCBS Edition). 2013e. www.accesstoinsight.org/tipitaka/mn/mn.062.than.html.

Ṭhānissaro Bhikkhu, translator. "Mettā (Mettānisamsa) Sutta: Good Will (AN 11.16)." Access to Insight (BCBS Edition). 2013a. www.accesstoinsight.org/tipitaka/an/an11/an11.016.than.html.

Ṭhānissaro Bhikkhu, translator. "The Road to Nirvana Is Paved with Skillful Intentions." Access to Insight (BCBS Edition). 2011. www.accesstoinsight.org/lib/authors/thanissaro/intentions.html.

Ṭhānissaro Bhikkhu, translator. "Sona Sutta: About Sona (AN 6.55)." Access to Insight (BCBS Edition). 2013f. www.accesstoinsight.org/tipitaka/an/an02/an02.031.than.html.

Thera, Nyanaponika, translator. "The Four Sublime States: Contemplations on Love, Compassion, Sympathetic Joy and Equanimity." Access to Insight (BCBS Edition). 2013. www.accesstoinsight.org/lib/authors /nyanaponika/wheel006.html.

Thera, Nyanaponika, translator. "Sallatha Sutta: The Dart (SN 36.6)." Access to Insight (BCBS Edition). 2010. www.accesstoinsight.org/tipitaka/sn /sn36/sn36.006.nypo.html.

Treleaven, David A. *Trauma-Sensitive Mindfulness: Practices for Safe and Transformative Healing.* New York: W. W. Norton, 2018.

Vajira, Sister, and Francis Story, translator. "Maha-parinibbana Sutta: Last Days of the Buddha (DN 16)." Access to Insight (BCBS Edition). 2013. www.accesstoinsight.org/tipitaka/dn/dn.16.1-6.vaji.html.

van der Kolk, Bissel A. *The Body Keeps the Score: Brain, Mind, and Body in the Healing of Trauma.* New York: Viking, 2014.

van Oers, H. A., L. Haverman, P. F. Limperg, E. M. van Dijk-Lokkart, H. Maurice-Stam, and M. A. Grootenhuis. "Anxiety and Depression in Mothers and Fathers of a Chronically Ill Child." *Maternal and Child Health Journal* 18:8 (2014). https://doi.org/10.1007 /s10995-014-1445-8.

Walshe, Maurice O'Connell, translator. "Attadiipaa Sutta: An Island to Oneself (SN 22.43)." Access to Insight (BCBS Edition). 2013. www.accesstoinsight.org/tipitaka/sn/sn22/sn22.043.wlsh.html.

Warren, Shantigarbha. "Steps to Mourning and Healing." Seeds of Peace YouTube Channel. 2018.

Weber, Akincano Marc. "Brahmavihārās, as Practices for the Relational World." Dharma Seed, July 3, 2017.

Weber, Akincano Marc. "Brahmavihārās: At the Heart of Human Experience." Dharma Seed, July 7, 2015.

Weber, Akincano Marc. "Hedonic Hotspots, Hedonic Potholes: Vedanā Revisited." *Contemporary Buddhism* 19:1 (2018), 7–30.

Weber, Akincano Marc. "Setting to Sea in the Leaky Boat of Self (Upadana)." Dharma Seed, July 14, 2014.

Weingast, Matty, translator. *The First Free Women: Original Poems Inspired by the Early Buddhist Nuns.* Boulder, CO: Shambhala, 2020.

Wilner, Paul, and Richard C. Goldstein. "Mediation of Depression by Perceptions of Defeat and Entrapment in High-Stress Mothers." *British Journal of Medical Psychology* 74:4 (2001), 473–85. https:// doi.org/10.1348/000711201161127.

World Health Organization. "The True Death Toll of COVID-19: Estimating Global Excess Mortality." 2022. www.who.int/data/stories /the-true-death-toll-of-covid-19-estimating-global-excess-mortality.

Yoshimura, Stephen M., and Kassandra Berzins. "Grateful Experiences and Expressions: The Role of Gratitude Expressions in the Link between Gratitude Experiences and Well-being." *Review of Communication* 17:2 (2017), 106–18. https://doi.org/10.1080/15358593.2017.1293836.

About the Author

Celia Landman is a mindfulness educator offering support to teens and adults. She draws from her range of experience working with folks impacted by trauma, addiction, and anxiety to create customized meditations, visualizations, and trainings that reconnect us to our wholeness. Mindfulness has brought greater happiness and stability to Celia's life, and her greatest aspiration is to help others recognize their true nature of love and ability. Celia Landman lives in Litchfield, Connecticut.

Monastics and visitors practice the art of mindful living in the tradition of Thich Nhat Hanh at our mindfulness practice centers around the world. To reach any of these communities, or for information about how individuals, couples, and families can join in a retreat, please contact:

Plum Village
33580 Dieulivol, France
plumvillage.org

Magnolia Grove Monastery
Batesville, MS 38606, USA
magnoliagrovemonastery.org

Blue Cliff Monastery
Pine Bush, NY 12566, USA
bluecliffmonastery.org

Deer Park Monastery
Escondido, CA 92026, USA
deerparkmonastery.org

**European Institute
of Applied Buddhism**
D-51545 Waldbröl, Germany
eiab.eu

Thailand Plum Village
Nakhon Ratchasima
30130 Thailand
thaiplumvillage.org

Asian Institute of Applied Buddhism
Ngong Ping, Lantau Island,
Hong Kong
pvfhk.org

Maison de l'Inspir
77510 Villeneuve-sur-Bellot, France
maisondelinspir.org

Healing Spring Monastery
77510 Verdelot, France
healingspringmonastery.org

Stream Entering Monastery
Beaufort, Victoria 3373, Australia
nhapluu.org

The Mindfulness Bell, a journal of the art of mindful living in the tradition of Thich Nhat Hanh, is published three times a year by our community. To subscribe or to see the worldwide directory of Sanghas, or local mindfulness groups, visit mindfulnessbell.org.

**PARALLAX
PRESS**

Parallax Press is a nonprofit publisher, founded and inspired by Zen Master Thich Nhat Hanh. We publish books on mindfulness in daily life and are committed to making these teachings accessible to everyone and preserving them for future generations. We do this work to alleviate suffering and contribute to a more just and joyful world. View our entire library at **parallax.org**.